Chicago, Burlington and Quincy

In Color

Volume 1
by Michael Spoor

Published by
Morning Sun Books, Inc.
11 Sussex Court
Edison, NJ 08820
Library of Congress Catalog Card Number: 94-075694
Layout and typesetting by R. J. Yanosey of Morning Sun Books, Inc.

First Printing
ISBN 1-878887-32-7

Dedication

*To my Mom and Dad who, when I was six years old, took me on the
train to visit my Grandparents in Kansas City. That train was the KANSAS
CITY ZEPHYR of the Chicago, Burlington and Quincy Railroad.*

Acknowledgements

Without the support of my wife, Monika, and our
son, Michael, I would not have attempted this
project. Once underway, they continued to provide
encouragement to keep going. Without them, this
book would have taken much longer. This book was
made possible because a number of photographers
who were trackside during the 1950s and 1960s to
capture on film the end of mainline steam and the
transition to diesels on the Burlington have made
their material available for this project. Excellent
photographers, Gib Allbach, the late Don Ball, the
late Paul Blough, R. W. Buhrmaster, Bob Bullermann, Barry Carlson, Joe Collias, the late Bernard
Corbin, Ed DeRouin, Jim Ewinger, Charles Franzen, Mike Gleason, the late K. C. Henkels, Michael
P. Joynt, George Kantola, Dave Lotz, Rod Master-
son, Jim Miller, the late Henry Page, Russ Porter,
Robert P. Olmsted, Karl Rethwisch, George Speir,
Hol Wagner, Dick Wallin, Richard Wolter, David
Van Drunen, the late Peter Van Drunen, Chuck
Zeiler, Harold Ziehr and Max Zimmerlein, have
shared their collections. The result is a book in
which none of the photographs have previously been
published. I express my most sincere thanks to all
of the above gentlemen.

Working with drawings and track charts, Bill
Edgar has created several of the maps that are used
in this book. I would like to thank to Bill for his
assistance. A special thanks to Jim Miller, a close
friend and past President of the Burlington Route
Historical Society, and Dave Lotz, another good
friend and current President of the BRHS for all of
the time spent assisting me in finding additional
photographs, researching the text and helping write
the introduction.

And finally, to all of my friends in the Burlington
Route Historical Society who have encouraged me
to undertake this project and, once underway, continued to support this effort by reviewing the
material, assisting with the technical information,
and helping me locate additional quality color
photography.

*The illustrations and timetables are from the col-
lections of Bob Bullermann, Jim Miller, George
Speir and Bob Yanosey, as well as my own.*

Chicago, Burlington and Quincy
In Color
Volume 1

Errata

- Two photos of CB&Q O-5A #5602 were inadvertently switched and printed on the wrong pages. The photo of #5602 on page 15 should be on page 125 and vice versa. The captions as they appear on those pages are correct.

...9 as the ...2 miles ...ilroad, ...o and ...d ac- AGO, ...DAD CO... ...ntil 186... ...me char... ...ake town... of the ...til 1901. ...'d westw... ...h Omaha... sidered... name f... used in t... the cent... the CB&... ern Pacifi... the Burli... ...iol of the Colorado & ... as well as the Ft. Worth and Denver City, heralding the arrival of the CB&Q to Ft. Worth, Dallas, Houston and Galveston on the Gulf of Mexico. The Burlington lines comprised 12,000 miles in fourteen states and truly ran "Everywhere West" of Chicago, but not west of the Rockies.

When most people think of the Chicago, Burlington and Quincy, they envision stainless steel passenger trains streaking across the farmlands of Illinois, Missouri and Iowa, or perhaps see the silver streamliners rolling along the eastern shore of the Mississippi, passing the wooden valleys, majestic palisades and frowning cliffs that profilerate along the Wisconsin side. When you mention the Burlington, many people think of the famous triple track "Racetrack" between Chicago and Aurora with its double deck commuter trains and lengthy steam and diesel powered time freights. Some will reflect on the rural heartland where the railroad moved the products of the farms and ranches to market. The trackage in the five states of Illinois, Iowa, Minnesota, Missouri and Wisconsin was officially called "Lines East of the Missouri River" and this is the CB&Q to be covered in this book.

The main focus of this color book is the motive power and trains of the Burlington immediately after World War II and into the early 1960s. This is that wonderful transition era when active steam was being phased out and replaced by diesel locomotives which were more efficient and less expensive to operate. The earliest color shots included in this book date back to November 1945.

While you will find examples of steam locomotives with eight different wheel arrangements in this book, the two most prominent classes are the O-5 Northerns and the M-4A Colorados. The 18 massive 2-10-4s, #6310-6327, were constructed inside the erecting halls of Baldwin at Eddystone, Pennsylvania from 1927 to 1929. Called "Colorados" by the Burlington, they would still be in active service in southern Illinois until late 1957.

The Burlington's very best steam locomotives were the 36 Class O-5 and O-5A Northerns. Baldwin built the first 8, #5600-5607, in 1930, while the railroad's West Burlington Shops constructed #5608-5635 from 1937 through 1940. These modern and efficient steam engines were commonly found on both passenger and freight assignments and were in mainline service until the end of steam.

After World War I, America embraced the automobile and took to the highways, with one of the results being diminished rail passenger travel, especially on the small branch lines. In the mid 1920s the Burlington, seeking operating efficiencies, accumulated the largest roster of gas-electric motor cars of any railroad in the country, many of which are included in this book. Eventually rostering 57 motor cars which were painted Pullman green with colorful red and yellow faces, these doodlebugs would be a fixture on the branch lines for 35 years. Perhaps more important than the immediate operating efficiencies they brought the Burlington, the motor cars provided the railroad with experience in handling internal combustion engines.

The Q purchased a diminutive four-wheel gas-electric switcher in 1929 from the Mack Truck Company. Numbered #100, it would spend most of its

life working the tie plant at Galesburg. It would be followed by a succession of small gas-electric switchers manufactured by Porter and Whitcomb. In 1933 the Burlington purchased its first diesel-electric switchers from Midwest Locomotive Works. Numbered #9121-9123, these 65-ton units heralded in the arrival of the diesels on the railroad.

Realizing the potential of the diesel-electric engine and having heard about a new concept of making passenger cars from stainless steel, utilizing a patented and revolutionary new process called "shotwelding," Burlington President Ralph Budd entered into discussions with the Edward G. Budd Manufacturing Company of Philadelphia to construct a stainless steel trainset. At the same time Ralph Budd turned to the Electro-Motive Company, which had been acquired by automobile manufacturer General Motors in 1930, to design and manufacture a diesel engine for railroad use. The result was an eight-cylinder, 600 horsepower engine. Given free hand by Ralph Budd, on April 7, 1934 the Budd Manufacturing Company unveiled the Burlington's new train - America's first diesel-powered streamlined train - the PIONEER ZEPHYR.

The superior performance of the diesel-electric ZEPHYRS convinced Burlington management to acquire additional diesel locomotives. With its close relationship with Electro-Motive, the CB&Q purchased two 900 hp EMD NW-1 locomotives in 1937. These were followed by eighteen 600 hp EMD SW-1 switchers, #9136-9153, which were delivered from June 1939 to February 1941 and eventually 45 1,000 hp NW-2 switchers which started arriving on the property in April 1940.

In March 1940, the railroad took delivery of its famous stainless steel EMC E-5A and E-5B passenger locomotives. These twelve 2,000 hp units, numbered variously from #9909-9915B, were only the beginning because they would be followed by 44 E-7As, 38 E-8As and 16 E-9As delivered between November 1945 and January 1956.

When World War II broke out, the War Production Board monitored the delivery of diesel locomotives to the nation's railroads. While the CB&Q wanted more EMC products, (Electro-Motive Division beginning January 1, 1941) the Board only allotted the railroad 30 Baldwin 1,000 hp VO-1000s and 10 Alco 1,000 hp S-2s, all of which were delivered during 1943 and 1944. Needing additional locomotives to move wartime tonnage, the Q received permission from the Board in 1943 to acquire 16 four-unit 5400 hp FT diesel freight locomotives. Numbered #100-115, all would be delivered between December, 1943 and September, 1944. After the war, the Q would return to EMD for multiple purchases of additional F-units, eventually accumulating a roster of 124 FTs, F-2s, F-3s and F-7s

for freight service and 9 F-3s for passenger service. While the fleet of F-units was expanding, the Burlington received another 20 EMD switchers in the summer of 1950, all were 1,200 hp SW-7s.

These would sound the deathnell for the remaining steam switchers left on the roster. In 1951, EMD would introduce the 1,500 hp general purpose roadswitcher which they called the GP-7. The CB&Q, an established EMD customer, bought 67 of these multiple purpose engines from 1951-1953. EMD enhanced its roadswitcher to 1,750 hp in 1954, designating this new model as a GP-9, and the Burlington acquired 20 of these, numbered #270-289. At the same time the roadswitcher was joining the roster, the Burlington was seeking a replacement for the venerable 2-10-4s that had proven so reliable on the lines in southern Illinois. EMD responded in 1953 with the six axle 1,500 hp SD-7 and in 1954 with the 1,750 hp SD-9. In 1953, the Q purchased 25 of the SD-7s, numbered #300-324, and in 1954 50 SD-9s, #325-374.

PATHFINDERS OF THE DIESEL ERA

The original Burlington Zephyr which inaugurated a new era in American transportation history in 1934. After more than 1,650,000 miles it still is assigned to its daily round trip of 465 miles between Lincoln and McCook, Nebraska.

Latest of the illustrious descendants of the original Zephyr—one of the sixteen 5400-horsepower General Motors Freight Locomotives being put into wartime service by the Burlington Lines.

Any book covering "Lines East" of the Chicago, Burlington and Quincy should start in Chicago and go "Everywhere West." West to Aurora, St. Paul, Galesburg, southern Illinois, Quincy, St. Louis, St. Joseph, Burlington, Pacific Junction and Council Bluffs. This volume of *CHICAGO BURLINGTON & QUINCY In Color* will concentrate only on steam and the first generation of diesels that replaced the iron horses. Another volume will follow with the classic "Chinese Red" second generation of diesels. Appropiately, our tour of "Lines East" begins at Chicago Union Station.

CHICAGO, BURLINGTON & QUINCY RAILROAD
Lines East of the Missouri River
Circa 1961

Main lines:
Secondary lines:
Trackage rights:
Lines west:

Map not to scale

Map drawn by W. R. Edgar, © Great Northern Graphics

PAGES	
	8-47
	48-59
	60-85
	86-95
	96-109
	110-128

Chicago, Burlington & Quincy Railroad Company
ASSIGNMENT OF LOCOMOTIVES AND MOTOR CARS, JUNE 1, 1954

LINES EAST

CHICAGO DIVISION — AURORA DIVISION

(1)	(2)	(3)	(4)
*F1 545	*G5 504	SW1 600HP 9140 ▴9153	@E5 4500HP AB
ƒ* S4 A s X4001	G5 A 511 512 515	NW2 1000HP ▴9208 ▴9209 9218 ▴9222 9226 9231 9233 9237 ▴9245 9247	s9938 s9939 s9940 s9941 s9942 s9943 s9945 s9946 s9947 s9948
ƒ* O1 A X4947	ƒ=* S4 s3000 3001 3003 3004 3005 3006 3010 s3012	SW7 1200HP s▴4000 ▴9256	SW1 600HP 9149 9150
NW1 900HP ▴9200 ▴9201	BLW 1000HP ▴9351 ▴9357 ▴9368 ▴9369 ▴9370 ▴9371 ▴9372 ▴9374 ▴9375 ▴9376 ▴9379	TR2 2000HP AB 9406 9407	NW2 1000HP 9207 9214 9216 9223 9248
NW2 1000HP ▴9212 ▴9213 ▴9220 ▴9221 ▴9224 ▴9227	ƒ* O5 A s X5616 s X5617 s X5618 s X5619 s X5624 s X5628 s X5634 s X5635	1200HP @9906B @9907B	@GP7 1500HP 203 235
ƒ* O1 A X4942 X4955 X4969 X4964 =4980 =4981 =4986 =6146	@GP7 1500HP ▴209 s243 s244	@GP7 1500HP 204 211 231 245 249 259	TR2 2000HP AB 9401 9411 9412 9413
ƒ* O5 A s X5615 s X5616 s X5617 s X5618 s X5619 s X5624 s X5628 s X5634 s X5635	@GP7 1500HP ▴209 @s243 s244	Exh. Eng. §5 1800HP 9904 9905 9906A 9907A	
@GP7 1500HP ▴209 s243 s244		@E5 2000HP s9913	
		@E7 s9917A s9931B s9937A	
		@E8 2250HP s9937B s9949A s9964 s9965 s9966 s9967 s9968 s9969 s9970 s9971 s9972 s9973 s9974 s9975 s9976 s9977	
		@E5 4000HP AB s9910 s9911 s9912 s9914 s9915	
		@E7 4000HP AB s9916 s9918 s9919 s9920 s9921 s9922 s9923 s9924 s9925 s9926 s9927 s9928 s9929 s9930	
		Zephyr 600HP @s9902	

CHICAGO DIVISION (diesel sets)

@E5 4000HP AB — %FT-F2 4050HP ABC — %FT 5400HP ABCD — %F3 4500HP ABC — %F3 6000HP ABCD

▴150 ▴151 ▴152 ▴153 ▴154 ▴155 ▴156 ▴157 ▴158 ▴159 203 235 ▴160 ▴161 162 163 164 165 166 167 168 169 ▴105 ▴106 ▴107 ▴108 ▴109 ▴110 ▴111 ▴112 ▴113 ▴114 ▴115 ▴116 ▴117 ▴118 ▴119 ▴120 ▴121 ▴122 ▴123 ▴124 ▴125 ▴126 ▴127 ▴128 ▴129 ▴130 ▴131 ▴132 ▴133 ▴134 ▴135 ▴136

La Crosse Division

ƒ* S4 A s=4004 — ƒ* O1 A =4998 — ƒ* O5 A s X5621 s X5622 s X5630 s X5631 X5633 — SW1 600HP 9150 — NW2 1000HP 9207 9214 9223 9248 — @GP7 1500HP 203 235 — TR2 2000HP AB 9401 9411 9412 9413

GALESBURG DIVISION

		Ottumwa Creston
G10 564 570 574 581	ƒ* M2 A =6126	K2 637
ƒ* S4 s3007	ƒ* M4 A X6316 X6317 X6318 X6321 X6323 X6325	ƒ* O3 =5345
ƒ* O1 A X4943 X4950 X4956 X4957 X4961 X4962 X4967 =4970 =4973 =4975 =4978 =4979 =4983 =4990 =4994 =4997 X5126	GE 400HP 9120	GE 280HP 8902
SW1 600HP 9148	Shop Eng. 308	DE 360HP 9103
NW2 1000HP 9205 9210 9215 9219 9243 9244	GE 280HP 8902	SW 600HP 9131
SW7 1200HP ▴9253 ▴9254 ▴9255 ▴9257 ▴9258 ▴9259 9260	DE 360HP 9104	SW1 600HP 9139
NW2 1000HP 9206	SW 600HP 9132 9135	NW2 1000HP 9211 9240 9243
@GP7 1500HP 200 201 202 206 215 216 229 233 237 238 239 240 248 251 252 255 257 265 267		
TR2 2000HP AB 9402 9403 9408 9409		
PMC 275HP 9732 9773 DE9816 9818 9848		
400HP DE9735 9766 DE9772		

Beardstown Division

*F1 543 546 549 — * S2 A X2905 — ƒ* O1 A X4940 X4945 X4951 =4952 X4960 X4963 X4966 X4968 =4972 =4988 =4991 =4992 =4993 =4996 =4999 =5096 =5118 X5140 =5144 — ƒ* M4 A =6310 =6311 =6312 =6313 =6314 =6315 X6319 X6320 X6322 X6324 X6326 X6327 — NW2 1000HP 9206 — @E7 275HP s9949 — @GP7 1500HP 219 — SD7 1500HP 401 402 403 404 405 406 407 — SW1 Creston Divn. 600HP ▴9145 ▴9146 — PMC 275HP 9731 DE9849 — Zephyr 600HP @9900 @9903 — Zephyr 1000HP @9908

Hannibal Division

SW 600HP 9130 9134 — SW1 600HP 9138 — NW2 1000HP 9217 ▴9225 9226 9230 ▴9235 9238 9239 9241 9246 — SW7 1200HP ▴9350 ▴9352 ▴9353 ▴9354 ▴9355 ▴9356 ▴9358 ▴9359 ▴9360 ▴9361 9362 9363 9364 9365 9366 9377 9378 — SW9 1200HP 9268 9269 9270 — @GP7 1500HP 207 252 259 261 262 263 264 266 — @E7 2000HP AB TR2 2000HP AB 9400 9404 9405 — PMC 275HP DE9841 DE9845

St. Joseph Division

DE 360HP 9106 — SW1 600HP 9123 — SW 600HP 9133 — SW1 600HP 9152 — BLW 1000HP 9122

LINES WEST

LINCOLN DIVISION — Omaha Division

	K4	§* O5 B	Wymore Division
G5 A 510 516	910 915	X6626 X6627 X6629 X6632	GE 275HP 9097
G10 ⊠579	K10 967	Shop Eng. 305	DE 360HP 9107
⊠ X4949 ⊠ =2863	* S2 A =2903	SW1 600HP 9137	SW1 600HP 9137
ƒ* O1 A ⊠ =5116 =5119 =5130 X5121	ƒ* O1 A X4958	SW7 1200HP 408 409 410 411	SD7 1500HP 400
DE 450HP 9122	§* S4 B ⊠=4002 =4003	Shop Eng. 304	SW7 1200HP 400 408 409 410 411
SW1 600HP 9141 9142 9144	⊠ X5112 ⊠ =5132 ⊠ =5136 ⊠ =5139	NW2 1000HP 9229	Shop Eng. 304
NW2 1000HP ▴9203 ▴9204 ▴9232 ▴9234 9236	ƒ* O3 X5515	ALCO 1000HP ▴9300 ▴9301 ▴9303 ▴9304 ▴9305 ▴9307 ▴9308	
SW7 1200HP ▴9268	@GP7 1500HP 205 212 214 218 221 223 226	Shop Eng. 311	
@GP7 1500HP 219 220 247	X5332 X5333 X5334 X5335 X5344 X5346 X5349 =5351 =5352 =5356 X5357	SW1 600HP 9143 9147	
SD7 1500HP 401 402 403 404 405 406 407		@GP7 1500HP 208 210 217 222 246	
@E7 2000HP s9917B		%@SD7 1500HP 318	
PMC 275HP 9726		TR2 2000HP AB ▴9410	
400HP DE9769 DE9770		@E7 2000HP s9931A	
SW1 Creston Divn. 600HP ▴9145 ▴9146		PMC 275HP 9730	

McCook Division

G10 ⊠578 — ƒ* O1 A ⊠ =4976 ⊠ =4996 X5090 X5092 X5138 X5143 — §* O5 B X5614 X5620 — Shop Eng. 304 — NW2 1000HP 9229 — ALCO 1000HP ▴9300 ▴9301 ▴9303 ▴9304 ▴9305 ▴9306 — SW1 600HP 9143 9147 — @GP7 1500HP 208 210 217 222 246 — %@SD7 1500HP 318 — @E7 2000HP s9917B — TR2 2000HP AB 9726 — 400HP DE9769 DE9770

ALLIANCE DIVISION — Sterling Division

G10 §565	§K4 919	%@SD7 1500HP 300 308 310 312 313 314 316 321 322 323 324
ƒ* O1 A ⊠ =5085	§G3 1653	
§* O4 X5500 =5503 X5504 =5505 =5506 X5509 X5513	* O1 A ⊠ X6072 ⊠# X6082 ⊠# X6084 ⊠# X6089	%@SD9 1750HP 325 326 327 328 329 330 331 332
§* O5 B X5614 X5620	§§ X5079 § X6079	
ƒ* M2 A ⊠ X6131 ⊠ =6147 ⊠ X6163	§ X5127 § X5129 § X5147	
X* B1 A §7014 §7018 §7019 §7020	§* O4 X5501 X5507 X5508	
ALCO 1000HP ▴9300 ▴9301 ▴9303 ▴9304 ▴9305 ▴9306	DE 360HP 9105	
SW1 600HP 9143 9147	%@SD7 1500HP 309 315 317	
@GP7 1500HP 208 210 217 222 246	%@SD9 1750HP 338 339 340 341 342 343 344	
%@SD7 1500HP 319	ALCO 1000HP 9302 9306	
%@SD9 1750HP 333 334 335 336 337	PMC 400HP DE9768	

CASPER DIVISION — Sheridan Division

%@SD7 1500HP 300 308 310 312 313 314 316 321 322 323 324 — %@SD9 1750HP 325 326 327 328 329 330 331 332 / Shop Eng. — GASO 90HP 8901

LEASED

@E5 Jt. Tex 2000HP 9909 — B & S *R4 A ⊠1987

Totals — LINES EAST

	Chicago Div.	Aurora	La Crosse	Galesburg	Ottumwa Creston	Beardstown	Hannibal	St. Joseph
Stm.	3	30	7	43	3	38	—	—
DE	24	131	13	40	6	34	34	32
PMC				8		2	2	2
Exh. Eng.		1				1		
Zep.		1						
GE					1			
Shop Eng.				2				
Tot.	**27**	**163**	**20**	**93**	**10**	**40**	**39**	**34**

Chicago Division		Galesburg		Beardstown	Hannibal	St. Joseph
Steam	40	Steam	46	Stm. 38	DE 34	DE 32
DE	168	DE	46	DE	PMC 2	PMC 2
Exh. Eng.	1	GE	1	PMC 1	Zep. 3	
Zephyr	1	PMC	8			
		Shop Eng.	2			
Total	**210**	**Total**	**103**	**Tot. 40**	**Tot. 39**	**Tot. 34**

Total Lines East: Steam 124 / DE 281 / GE 1 / PMC 13 / Shop Eng. 2 / Exh. Eng. 1 / Zep. 4 — **Total 426**

Totals — LINES WEST

	Lincoln (Omaha)	K4	McCook	Alliance	Sterling	Casper	Sheridan	Leased
Stm.	28	—	—	16	13	—	—	1
DE	23	7	—	11	11	11	8	1
GE		1						
PMC	3			1	1			
Shop Eng.	1			1			Shop Eng. 1	
Tot.	**55**	**8**		**29**	**25**	**11**	**9**	**2**

Lincoln Division		McCook		Alliance		Casper	
Steam	28	Stm.	10	Steam	29	DE	19
DE	30	DE	24	DE	22	Shop Eng.	1
GE	1	PMC	1	Shop Eng.	1		
PMC	3	Shop Eng.	1	PMC	2		
Shop Eng.	1	Stm. 8 / DE 22 / Tot. 30					
Tot.	**63**	**Tot 36**		**Total 54**		**Total 20**	

Total Lines West: Steam 75 / DE 117 / GE 1 / PMC 6 / Shop Eng. 4 — **Total 203**

---

*SUPERHEATER §OIL BURNER ƒSTOKER ⊠L & B FRONT END ▴RADIO ▪AUTOMATIC TRAIN CONTROL XWORTHINGTON, =ELESCO—FEED WATER HEATERS

DE—DIESEL-ELECTRIC   GE—GAS-ELECTRIC   S—CAB SIGNALS   @STEAM BOILER   %DYNAMIC BRAKES

Chicago Union Station

The original Chicago Union Station, located at Canal and Adams Streets, opened in 1881 and was replaced by the current structure in July 1925. The Chicago, Burlington and Quincy Railroad was one of Chicago Union Station's four owners and used its facilities since its opening. The Burlington shared the fifteen tracks on the south side of the station with the Pennsylvania Railroad and the Gulf, Mobile & Ohio, while the tracks on the north side were used exclusively by the Milwaukee Road.

(Left) The Burlington inaugurated diesel powered, lightweight, stainless steel, air-conditioned, overnight passenger service between Chicago and Denver in November 1936 when the DENVER ZEPHYR began operations. The articulated train was replaced in October 1956 with new full size Budd-built stainless steel cars to completely re-equip the DENVER ZEPHYR. Operating westbound as Train #1, the DZ was the flag-ship of the ZEPHYR fleet. Built by Budd for DZ service, here Vista-Dome parlor-observation *Silver Chateau* patiently awaits its 5:00 p.m. departure. *(George Speir)*

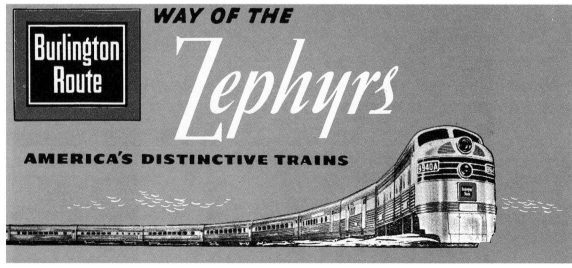

Offering the most comfortable train travel possible, the CALIFORNIA ZEPHYR provided an unequalled scenic experience on its three day voyage from Chicago to San Francisco. Choreographed to pass through the Colorado Rockies and California's Feather River Canyon during daylight, the CALIFORNIA ZEPHYR's schedule called for it to pull away from the bumpers of Chicago Union Station at 3:30 p.m. *(George Speir)*

Roosevelt Road

Just a few blocks south of Chicago Union Station, the Roosevelt Road viaduct crossed over the approaches to the station to the north and the coach yards to the south. Always a railfan paradise, the Roosevelt Road viaduct was an unsurpassed location to photograph the trains of the Burlington, Pennsylvania and Gulf, Mobile & Ohio.

(Left) Departing CUS at 11:35 A.M. and passing under Roosevelt Road at 11:40 A.M., Train #115, a mid-day suburban train, is under control of #9937B, the Burlington's first EMD E-8A which had been delivered in December 1949. After the arrival of the Budd-built stainless steel bilevel suburban cars in 1950, the consist of the mid-day suburban service trains was usually one power car and one of the bilevels. The E-8A still has the original full skirts on the fuel tanks and the coupler cover but the stainless steel side panels were installed by the shop crew at the West Burlington diesel shops subsequent to the locomotive's delivery.
(R. P. Olmsted, M. Spoor collection)

(Below) Because of its afternoon arrival and departure from Chicago Union Station, the Burlington's CALIFORNIA ZEPHYR was always a favorite of photographers. Inbound Train #18 has just passed under Roosevelt Road and is only a few minutes away from its scheduled 2:05 p.m. arrival. On this day in August 1965, the CZ has a Chesapeake & Ohio sleeper cut in just ahead of dome-observation *Silver Solarium. (M. Spoor collection)*

(Right) CB&Q E-8A #9964 leads the eastbound CALIFORNIA ZEPHYR past the Pennsylvania and Burlington coach yards and is about to go underneath Roosevelt Road. In a few minutes, Train #18 will be at the bumpers at Chicago Union Station and will have completed its three day journey from Oakland, California. The lead motor this day, June 21, 1958, is the first locomotive from the Burlington's third order of EMD E-8s and the first to come from the manufacturer with stainless steel side panels.
(R. P. Olmsted, M. Spoor collection)

...the California Zephyr

A. COTSWORTH, Jr.
Passenger Traffic Manager
547 West Jackson Blvd.
Chicago 6, Illinois

H. F. ENO
Passenger Traffic Manager
1531 Stout Street
Denver 1, Colorado

JOSEPH G. WHEELER
Passenger Traffic Manager
526 Mission Street
San Francisco 5, California

WESTBOUND—The Zephyr leaves Chicago in mid-afternoon, arrives Denver about breakfast-time next morning, glides through the mighty Rockies and reaches Salt Lake City that evening. Next morning it enters California through Beckwourth Pass, in the heart of the majestic Sierra Nevada, then traverses the spectacular Feather River Canyon. Oakland, San Francisco and the Golden Gate are reached in the afternoon.

EASTBOUND—The Zephyr leaves San Francisco in the morning, passes through the Feather River Canyon and the Sierra before dusk and arrives at Salt Lake City in the early morning. After a glorious trip through the Rockies, Denver is reached in the evening and Chicago soon after noon the following day.

(Right) Looking south from Roosevelt Road provides a panoramic view of the Burlington's 14th Street Coach Yard. This mid-morning view finds the suburban fleet at rest awaiting the call for the afternoon rush hour to the western suburbs.
(Bob Bullermann)

On August 14, 1943, the Burlington placed an order with the Baldwin Locomotive Works for six of its VO-1000 1,000 hp diesel-electric switchers. This order was increased to eight units in October 1943, and eventually to 30 locomotives. By December, 1944, the entire fleet of 30 Baldwins was on the property. They would be the only Baldwin products purchased by the Burlington. Beginning in November 1944, many of them were assigned to Chicago. Numbered in the series #9350-9379, a number of the VO-1000s would spend much of their lives toiling away at Chicago Union Station and the Coach Yard at 14th Street. For commuters, intercity passengers and railfans, they were a common sight at 14th Street and would finally be retired during the first quarter of 1967.

(Above) On a summer day in June 1960, VO-1000 #9372 is seen pulling a cut of passenger cars out of Chicago Union Station and past the Harrison Street Tower. In a few minutes it will be in the Coach Yard at 14th Street. Immediately ahead of #9372 is the Burlington's office car *Aleutian,* and in front of it is one of the 300-series diner-parlor-observations. Built by Pullman in 1923, the Burlington acquired the *Aleutian* in October, 1940 and subsequently refurbished it in 1952. Missouri Portland Cement Co. which bought it from the CB&Q in 1966, eventually donated the car to the National Museum of Transport in St. Louis where it is still on display and lettered *Barrets Station.* *(George Speir)*

Form 2573

TRAIN PORTER'S CHECK · Burlington Route

To: STATION TAXICAB STAND

No. 324229

From:

SPACE	CAR	TRAIN	DATE

PASSENGER'S DUPLICATE CHECK

PLEASE PRESENT TO RED CAP AT STATION TAXICAB STAND PROMPTLY ON ARRIVAL OF THIS TRAIN.

USUAL RED CAP SERVICE CHARGE WILL APPLY.

It is agreed that the carrier's liability is limited to not more than $50 for the article of hand baggage or other personal effects, including contents, covered by this receipt unless a greater value is declared in writing on form provided for that purpose.

No. 324229 · Burlington Route

Route of the Vista Dome Zephyrs

(Right) VO-1000 #9372 moves into the 14th Street Coach Yard with a string of Great Northern cars. The idle heavyweight Pullmans in the Pennsylvania coach yard in the background will rarely see any more revenue service since, when this photo was taken in May 1966, heavy train discontinuances would make the older equipment surplus. *(Bob Bullermann)*

(Left) Pushing a suburban service power car towards Chicago Union Station on a summer day in June 1964, VO-1000 #9367 rolls past a string of express cars stored in the Pennsylvania Railroad coach yard. The head end equipment on the storage track includes Pennsylvania X-29 express boxcars, New Haven express cars converted from U.S. Army troop sleepers and Railway Express Agency express refrigerators built in 1957. *(Bob Bullermann)*

(Right) On the same June day in 1964, another Baldwin VO-1000, #9379, is backing out of Chicago Union Station and is headed back to 14th Street. This overhead shot provides an excellent look at the wagonwheel antenna, auxiliary generator and equipment box which were mounted on top of most of the Burlington's the VO-1000s. The building in the background is part of the Railway Express Agency complex. *(Bob Bullermann)*

Hawthorne Yard

The Burlington first purchased land for a freight yard in the Chicago area in 1880. The original yard, completed in 1889 and called Hawthorne, would be elevated with fill from 1906 to 1908. In 1917, a young engineer named Harry C. Murphy, who would later become President of the Railroad in September 1949, helped to lay out the new eastbound yard that would be operational in 1918. By 1919 the new westbound yard was in service and both facilities would remain relatively unchanged until the late 1950s.

Chicago, Burlington & Quincy Railroad Company
LINES EAST OF THE MISSOURI RIVER

TIME TABLE

OF THE
CHICAGO AND AURORA DIVISIONS
OF THE
EASTERN DISTRICT

No. 35

EFFECTIVE AT 12:01 A. M. CENTRAL STANDARD TIME
SUNDAY, APRIL 27, 1952
DESTROY ALL TIME TABLES OF PREVIOUS DATE

This Time Table is for the exclusive use and guidance of the employes concerned, who must carry in addition thereto the Book of Rules of the Operating Department.

Distance from Chicago	STATIONS
0.	CHICAGO UNION STATION
	1.72
1.72	HALSTED STREET
	2 00
3.72	WESTERN AVENUE
	3.16
6.88	CICERO
	0.58
7.46	MORTON PARK
	1.01
8.47	CLYDE
	0 56
9.03	LA VERGNE
	0 54
9.57	BERWYN
	0.48
10.05	HARLEM AVENUE
	0.96
11.01	RIVERSIDE
	0 73
11.74	HOLLYWOOD
	0 53
12.27	BROOKFIELD
	0.75
13.02	CONGRESS PARK
	0.73
13.75	LA GRANGE
	0.39
14.14	STONE AVENUE
	1 24
15.38	WESTERN SPRINGS
	0 92
16.30	HIGHLANDS
	0.53
16.83	HINSDALE
	0.93
17.76	WEST HINSDALE
	0.48
18.24	CLARENDON HILLS
	1 16
19.40	WESTMONT
	0.90
20.30	FAIRVIEW AVENUE
	0.82
21.12	DOWNERS GROVE
	1.44
22.56	BELMONT
	1.84
24.40	LISLE
	4.04
28.44	NAPERVILLE
	4.98
33.42	EOLA
	1.85
35.27	WEST EOLA
	2.49
37.76	AURORA
	SCHEDULE TIME
	AVERAGE MILES PER HOUR

CHICAGO AND AURORA DIVISIONS
TIME TABLE No. 35.

In 1930 the Chicago, Burlington & Quincy received eight 4-8-4 steam locomotives from Baldwin which the railroad designate Class O-5 and numbered #5600-5607. These locomotives were purchased for fast freight service on the busy Chicago-Galesburg-Lincoln-Denver mainline. Highly pleased with the performance of the initial batch of O-5 engines, the Burlington would build an additional 28 similiar engines in its shops at West Burlington, Iowa over the next ten years. These would bear the class designation O-5A. When the struggle against the Axis began in 1941, the Burlington would have 36 Class O-5 and O-5A 4-8-4s available to handle wartime fast freight, troop trains and passenger assignments.

(Opposite page, top) In April 1952 the third of the original O-5 engines, #5602, is moving through the yard in Cicero. *(Don Ball Collection)*

(Opposite page, bottom) During 1952 and 1953 the Burlington installed cab signals and Mars lights on a number of steam locomotives assigned to Lines East. In this photo taken on September 28, 1956, Class O-5A #5605, having just arrived on an eastbound freight from Galesburg, is at the ash pit at Clyde Yard. The Mars light above the headlight and cab signal equipment mounted on the boiler are both clearly visible. This equipment had been added to #5605 in August 1952. *(R.W. Buhrmaster)*

Cicero's Automatic Classification Yard

With the growth of freight traffic through the Chicago terminal area, railroad management decided in 1955 that the yard in Cicero had to be revamped and mechanized to the greatest extent possible. A delegation of Burlington engineering and operating officials made several trips to visit hump yards in the East and South for pointers on what facilities to use at Cicero. The Q also drew on its own experiences during World War II in constructing hump retarder yards at Lincoln, Nebraska and Galesburg, Illinois. In effect, an entirely new yard was created at Cicero. Practically every track was moved, including the main lines which were moved north to allow for the new hump. Included in this project was the construction of seven new buildings, not including the Clyde diesel shop which had been built in the 1940s. The entire Cicero Automatic Classification Yard project was fully completed and put in service in 1958.

Map Showing Major
BURLINGTON FACILITIES
Along The Route Of
Your Tour To
THE NEW
CICERO AUTOMATIC CLASSIFICATION YARD

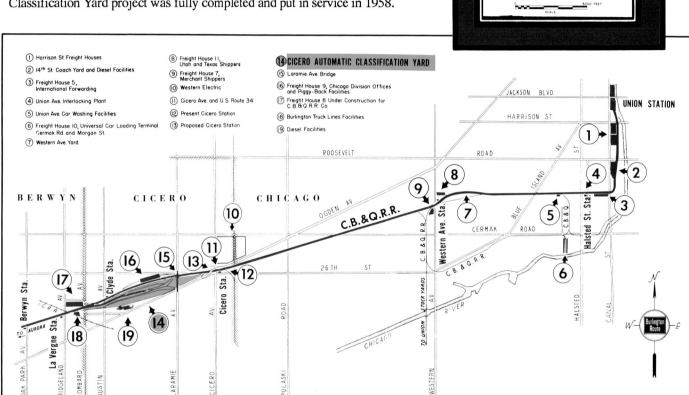

1. Harrison St. Freight Houses
2. 14th St. Coach Yard and Diesel Facilities
3. Freight House 5, International Forwarding
4. Union Ave. Interlocking Plant
5. Union Ave. Car Washing Facilities
6. Freight House 10, Universal Car Loading Terminal Cermak Rd. and Morgan St.
7. Western Ave. Yard
8. Freight House 11, Utah and Texas Shippers
9. Freight House 7, Merchant Shippers
10. Western Electric
11. Cicero Ave. and U.S. Route 34
12. Present Cicero Station
13. Proposed Cicero Station
14. CICERO AUTOMATIC CLASSIFICATION YARD
15. Laramie Ave. Bridge
16. Freight House 9, Chicago Division Offices and Piggy-Back Facilities
17. Freight House 8 Under Construction for C.B.&Q.R.R. Co.
18. Burlington Truck Lines Facilities
19. Diesel Facilities

(Left) A number of different types of switch engines worked the yard at Cicero. You could always find several of the EMD NW-2s working the receiving, departing and classification yards. Here, on March 14, 1965, NW-2 #9221 is seen working the west end of the yard and is crossing over Austin Boulevard. *(Chuck Zeiler)*

(Above) The Baldwin VO-1000s were also a common sight at the Cicero Yard for over thirty years. From their delivery to the Burlington in 1944 until they were retired in 1967, a number of these switchers had always called Cicero home. VO-1000 #9370, switching the east end of Cicero Yard on January 6, 1961, had only six more years to work for the Burlington before being traded to General Electric in March 1967. This engine would end up spending one year working on the Atlantic Coast Line before being retired and scrapped in 1968. *(M. Spoor collection)*

(Above) In December 1963, #9372 is back in Cicero and is assigned to working the freight yard. Perhaps a less glamorous assignment than assembling ZEPHYRS in the Coach Yard at 14th Street, it would spend its last four years moving cars around Cicero, dragging transfer runs to the other Chicago area yards and readying freights to head "Everywhere West" before being retired in March 1967. *(George Speir)*

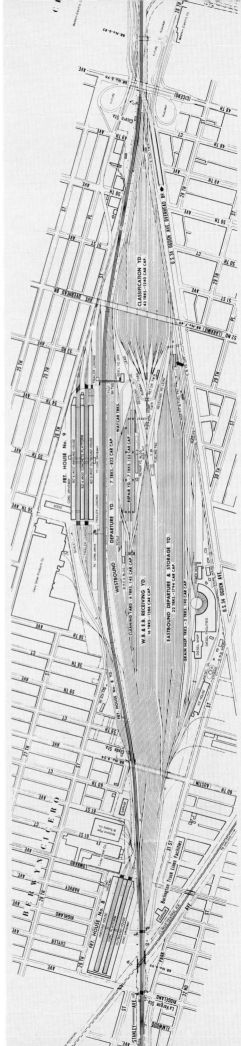

Cicero's NW-1 Switchers

Having acquired three Midwest centercab 450 hp switchers in 1933-1934, and subsequently five General Electric 360 hp switchers in 1940-1941, the Burlington turned to Electro-Motive Corporation in 1937 for six model SW 600 hp switchers. Pleased with the initial performance and cost savings of its small diesel switcher fleet, in late 1937 the Q was willing to try a newer model EMC switcher that developed 900 hp and accordingly acquired two NW-1s in November and December, 1937. Numbered #9200-9201, these two units featured a V-12 Winton 201A engine and General Electric transmissions and traction motors. With three small louvers at the top front side of each side of the hood and two exhaust stacks centered on the top of the hood, the two NW-1s represented the smallest class of diesel switch engines on the Burlington. When delivered, #9200 and 9201 were assigned to Hawthorne Yard in Cicero where they would spend most of their careers. They would also spend time at the yard at Western Avenue and at the Coach Yard at 14th Street. After spending twenty eight years tolling away at Hawthorne Yard and Cicero's automatic classification yard, both units would be sent back to EMD as trade-ins in the summer of 1965.

(Below) Only four months past its twenty fourth birthday, NW-1 #9201 is working the east end of the classification yard at Cicero on March 27, 1962. The three small louvers on the top front side of the hood are clearly visible. This photo was taken from Ogden Avenue, located on the south side of the classification yard, and provides an unobstructed view of the switch crews at work. *(K. C. Henkels, M. Spoor collection)*

(Top) This fireman's side view provides a good view of the three small louvers as well as the wagonwheel antenna and the unique illuminated number plates that stuck out in front of the headlight. NW-1 #9200, working the yard at Cicero in February 1964, is seen here waiting for its next assignment.
(George Speir)

(Center) On a cold, wintery March 28, 1965, NW-1 #9200 rests between assignments at the Clyde roundhouse. The unique illuminated number plates, found only on the two NW-1s, were mounted on the back of the cab as well as on the front headlight.
(Chuck Zeiler)

(Bottom) When this photo was taken on June 27, 1965, #9201 had less than one more month to work at Cicero before it would be traded to EMD for a new SW-1200 switcher. Here it is seen west of the Clyde diesel shop; just to the right is the ice plant of City Products Corporation.   *(Chuck Zeiler)*

FT to F2

(Top) On a hot August day in 1963, FT-A #113A and companion FT-B #113C hustle through Hollywood with eastbound tonnage bound for Cicero. Bearing built dates in August 1944, these units were part of the initial order for diesel freight locomotives that helped dieselize the Burlington and retire the iron horse. After completing twenty years of service, both would be retired in 1964 and traded in on new EMD GP-35s. *(George Speir)*

(Bottom) F-2A #155C was waiting for its next call to duty when photographed on Independence Day 1961. Well-maintained and having just turned fifteen years old, #155C had been delivered in July 1946 as one of the Q's ten F-2As. In ten months it would be traded in on a second generation GP-30, oddly not lasting as long as its elder FT cousin pictured above. *(M. Spoor collection)*

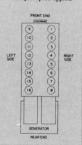

GENERAL DESCRIPTION

The freight locomotive consists of two or more units rated at 1350 H.P. each. The units with the cab will be known as "A" units, those without the cab as "B" units. Each unit has one 16-cylinder Diesel engine, a direct current generator and four traction motors. From each power plant the power is distributed to the traction motors which are mounted on the trucks. The traction motors are geared to the axle through spur gears. The units are electrically independent of each other except for certain low voltage wiring. Some of the "B" units have no batteries and are dependent on the "A" unit for this service.

The engines are "V" type with a 45° angle between banks and have a compression ratio of 16 to 1. Solid unit injection is employed, there being an injector centrally located in each cylinder head. The engines have a speed range of 275 to 800 R.P.M. Their speed is controlled by an electro-pneumatic governor control which is operated by the engineer's throttle. In this way all engines in the locomotive are controlled simultaneously. Each notch on the engineer's throttle changes the engine speed approximately 75 R.P.M.

The accompanying sketch serves to identify the cylinder locations, ends and sides of the engine, as they are referred to in this manual. The governor, electro-pneumatic governor control, water pumps and lubricating oil pumps are mounted on the "FRONT END." The blowers, oil separator and generator are mounted on the "REAR END."

Beginning in September 1951, the Burlington acquired a fleet of 68 EMD GP-7 1500 hp road switchers, with the last unit arriving on the property in December 1953. All of these units were delivered without dynamic brakes and were outfitted with Mars lights on both ends. Most were equipped with a steam generator for use on short passenger trains. These general purpose units, numbered #200-267, were commonly seen in yard service, local freight, secondary passenger and mainline freight service.

(Top) The Burlington's GP-7s were delivered in three groups. Burlington #209, a Phase I GP-7 delivered as part of the first group (#200-239) in September 1951, spent the first year of its life in Chicago-Downers Grove suburban service. Here it is working the classification yard in Cicero on August 4, 1966. The Q's GP-7s came with a full set of multiple unit connections.
(K. C. Henkels, M. Spoor collection)

(Center) The second batch, delivered in November 1952 and assigned numbers #240-252, were all Phase II locomotives. As such they were the first GPs to come with the oval slots located on the frame above the fuel tanks. On May 2, 1963 GP-7 #251 is moving through the Cicero classification yard.
(K.C. Henkels, M. Spoor collection)

(Bottom) The final 15 GP-7s, numbered #253-267, arrived in December 1953. Built as Phase II GP-7s, the engines in this group were identical to the 1952 engines. The GP-7s were a common sight at Cicero and could always be found working the yards or in transfer service to one of the other yards in Chicago. Here #259 pushes a string of cars in the classification yard on September 12, 1962. *(M. Spoor collection)*

Chicago to Aurora Suburban Service

The thirty eight miles from Chicago Union Station to Aurora is the best known portion of the CB&Q. Beginning in 1849 as the Aurora Branch Railroad, the Burlington has been an integral part of the development of Chicago's western suburbs. The Q's mainline passes through 14 suburban communities before arriving in Aurora. Suburban service trains have carried commuters to work and back home since the first line was opened in 1864. The early suburban trains were pulled by 4-4-0 steam locomotives and later supplemented by 0-6-2Ts. These tiny tank engines, of which there were only five and were designated Class I-1, were built from 1889-1893 and are the reason the suburban service trains are called "dinkies." These were in turn replaced by heavier 4-6-0 steam locomotives in classes K-1, K-2 and K-10, as well as Class P-6 and P-6A 4-4-2s. Beginning in 1926, the older wooden suburban service cars were replaced by rebuilt steel-plated cars and by new all-steel cars. By 1930 Pacifics drew this assignment and would hold this service until replaced by diesels in September 1952.

(Below) Class S-1A Pacific #2855, in charge of eastbound suburban Train #220, is crossing the Des Plaines River Bridge at Riverside, Illinois in November 1945. The open platform coach is one of the 7000-series suburban cars rebuilt in 1926-1927. *(Paul Blough, Bob Bullermann collection)*

(Top) Mid-day four car westbound Train #115, powered by Class S-2A #2948, is near Brookfield in this November 1945 photo. Some of the dinkies would carry baggage, newspapers and express and this day the first car of Train #115 is one of the five suburban service 3600-series combines.
(Paul Blough, Bob Bullermann collection)

— WEEK DAY TRAINS — WESTBOUND

WESTBOUND	223	133	135 Ex. Sat.	137 Ex. Sat. only	225 Ex. Sat.	139 Ex. Sat.	141 Ex. Sat.	229 Ex. Sat.	143 Ex. Sat.	145	211	147 Ex. Sat.	149	5	233	153	235	155	47	237	3	157	51	49	239	101
CHICAGO	PM	PM	PM	PM	PM	PM	PM	PM	PM	PM	PM	PM	PM	PM	PM	PM	PM	PM	PM	PM	PM	PM	PM	PM	PM	AM
Lv. Union Sta. Lv.	4 55	5 00	5 05	5 05	5 08	5 15	5 18	5 22		5 24	5 27	5 50	5 55	6 00	6 20	6 45	7 45	8 46	9 00	9 45	10 15	10 45	10 45	11 15	11 59	1 00
Halsted St. (at 16th)	5 00	5 05	5 10	5 10	5 13	5 20	5 23			5 29	5 32	5 55	6 00		6 25	6 50	7 50	8 50		9 50		10 50			12 05	1 05
Western Ave.	5 04	5 09	5 14	5 14	5 17	5 24				5 33	5 36	5 53	6 04		6 29	6 54	7 54	8 54		9 54		10 54			12 09	1 09
Cicero	5 09	5 14	5 19	5 19	5 22	5 30			5 38	5 41			6 09		6 34	6 59	7 59	8 59		9 59		10 59			12 14	1 14
Morton Park										5 43			6 11		6 36	7 01	8 01	9 01		10 01		11 01			12 16	1 16
Clyde						5 34				5 45			6 13		6 38	7 03	8 03	9 03		10 03		11 03			12 18	1 18
La Vergne						5 36				5 47			6 15		6 40	7 05	8 05	9 05		10 05		11 05			12 20	1 20
Berwyn				5 24		5 38				5 49		6 07	6 17		6 42	7 07	8 07	9 07		10 07		11 07			12 22	1 22
Harlem Ave.				5 26					5 44	5 51			6 19		6 44	7 09	8 09	9 09		10 09		11 09			12 24	1 24
Riverside			5 29	5 29	5 30					5 47		6 03	6 21		6 46	7 11	8 11	9 11		10 11		11 11			12 26	1 26
Hollywood			5 31							5 49	g		6 23		6 48	7 13	8 13	9 13		10 13		11 13			12 28	1 28
Brookfield			5 33			5 46							6 25		6 50	7 15	8 15	9 15		10 15		11 15			12 30	1 30
Congress Park			5 35			5 48				5 55			6 27		6 52	7 17	8 17	9 17		10 17		11 17			12 32	1 32
La Grange, La Grange Road		g	5 29	5 38	5 35			5 43	5 54	5 57		g	6 15	6 29	n	6 55	7 19	8 20	9 19	y	10 20		11 19			12 35	1 34
La Grange, Stone Ave.		5 26		5 40				5 46	5 56		g		6 31		6 57	7 21	8 22	9 21		10 22		11 21			12 37	1 36
Western Springs			5 33	5 43		5 40		5 42	5 48		6 01		6 34		7 00	7 24	8 25	9 24		10 25		11 24			12 40	1 39
Highlands				5 45			5 46					6 10	6 36		7 03	7 27	8 28	9 27		10 28		11 27			12 43	1 42
Hinsdale		5 31		5 47	5 42							6 12	6 39		7 05	7 29	8 30	9 29		10 30		11 29			12 45	1 44
West Hinsdale				5 49			5 56	5 48			6 07		6 41		7 07	7 31	8 32	9 31		10 32		11 31			12 47	1 46
Clarendon Hills				5 51			5 58	5 50			6 09		6 43		7 09	7 33	8 34	9 33		10 34		11 33			12 49	1 48
Westmont			5 39	5 53				5 54			6 12		6 46		7 12	7 36	8 37	9 36		10 36		11 36			12 52	1 51
Downers Grove, Fairview Ave.			5 42	5 57				5 57		6 09		6 35	6 48		7 14	7 38	8 39	9 38		10 39		11 38			12 54	1 53
Downers Grove, Main St.		5 40	5 45	6 00	6 06				6 09	6 12	6 15	6 20	6 38	6 50	7 17	7 40	8 42	9 44		10 42		11 40			12 57	1 55
Belmont	5 29			5 53			6 07					6 23			7 20		8 45			10 45					1 00	
Lisle	5 34			5 56			6 10					6 27			7 24		8 49			10 49					1 04	
Naperville	5 41			6 03			6 17					6 33			7 31		8 56			10 56					1 11	
Eola	5 47						6 22								7 37		9 02			11 02					1 17	
Ar. Aurora Ar.	5 55			6 15			6 30					6 45		6 50	7 45		9 10		11 05	11 10			11 33	12 03	1 25	
	PM	PM	PM	PM	PM	PM	PM	PM	PM	PM	PM	PM	PM	PM	PM	PM	PM	PM	PM	PM	PM	PM	AM	AM	AM	

(Bottom) Class S-2A #2948 is westbound at Hollywood with another mid-day train during November 1945. Built by Baldwin in 1910 and rebuilt to an S-2A in 1924, #2948 was a long-time suburban service engine which was one of many Pacifics assigned to suburban service beginning in 1929 simply because they had no other work on the Q. They had been bumped from the local passenger jobs by the new motor cars and from the mainline trains by the new Class S-4 Hudsons. An early victim of the arrival of the EMD E-7s, #2948 was stripped of usable parts and stored at Eola Yard near Aurora in June 1949. It was sold for scrap in May 1951.
(Paul Blough, Bob Bullermann collection)

Modernization of Suburban Service

After World War II, the Burlington's suburban service was faced with a number of challenges. The commuter equipment was old and not air-conditioned, while the motive power roster consisted of coal burning Pacifics. There were more commuters, which bode well for ridership, but the facilities at 14th Street could not be expanded to handle a larger fleet of commuter equipment. Longer trains were not the answer since the platforms at the suburban stations could not handle trains of greater length. Running more trains was not financially feasible. How does one modernize equipment, increase ridership, stabilize roster size and maintain current train lengths? In 1948 management embarked on a program to improve suburban equipment and to dieselize the suburban service. Seventy-nine all-steel suburban

coaches would be modernized and air-conditioned at the Aurora shops, of which 39 would be completed in 1949 and the remaining 40 in 1950. Sufficient diesel-electric locomotives from EMD would arrive between 1949 and 1951 to retire the last of the old Pacifics. The most innovative step taken in 1948 was placing an order with the Budd Company for 30 stainless-steel, air-conditioned gallery-type cars.

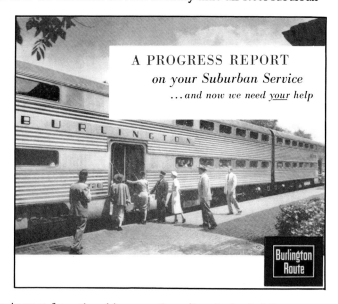

The Burlington's gallery cars ushered in the era of double-decked commuter equipment. These cars were a conventional 85 feet long, but the double-decked design resulted in each car being able to carry 148 passengers versus 98 in the older steel cars, with double seating on the main floor for 96 passengers and single seats for 52 passengers in the balconies. Trainmen could easily handle tickets of passengers in the balcony from the main floor. To differentiate the new stainless-steel equipment from the older cars, the railroad adopted the name Suburbanaire Service for all of the promotional material. The first gallery car arrived in August 1950, with the thirtieth car delivered in January, 1951. When placed in service, they had no individual power source and thus had to operate with a rebuilt and modernized coach that had been equipped with a diesel engine and electric generator.

(Left) E-8A #9941B powers westbound suburban service Train #223 through LaGrange in July 1958. Train #223, having left Chicago Union Station at 2:35 p.m. and scheduled to arrive in La-Grange at 3:04 p.m., was one of the mid-day trains which usually ran with one of the power cars and one or two gallery cars. The power cars outshopped by the Aurora shops during 1950-1951 were of two types: the suburban service generator/baggage coaches were numbered 7300-7301, while the generator/coaches were assigned #7302-7313. *(George Speir)*

THEN Remember "the good old days"—when your Burlington suburban train looked like this? Even then, the Burlington was regarded as a leader in suburban service. But there was room for improvement—and Burlington made those improvements.

NOW Here's the sleek diesel-powered suburban train of today... cool air-conditioning in the summer, warm in winter, clean and dependable all year 'round. No wonder Burlington suburban trains are widely recognized as tops in commutation travel.

The gallery cars were an instant success with commuters and additional cars were ordered throughout the 1950s, bringing the roster of stainless-steel gallery cars to 60 by 1958.

Burlington Route

EFFECTIVE
APRIL 27, 1958
Chicago Daylight Saving Time

EASTBOUND

Suburban Service

Union Passenger Station
CANAL AT JACKSON BLVD.
Phone FRanklin 2-6700

City Ticket Office
Bankers Building
ADAMS AT CLARK ST.
Phone WAbash 2-2345

(Above) An afternoon westbound suburban train is stopped at the platform in LaGrange in May 1960. E-9A #9985A is doing the honors this day and its 2400 hp will have no difficulty with the normal rush hour consist of a power car and 8-9 gallery cars. Built by EMD in December 1955, #9985A was delivered with stainless steel side panels, black nose stripes and the Burlington standard passenger-style pilot with coupler cover, which had been removed by the time this photo was taken.
(George Speir)

Chicago-Aurora Mainline

LaGrange

Once west of the yard at Cicero, the Burlington's famous triple track mainline, known to many railfans as the "Racetrack," passes through a succession of communities which trace their growth and prosperity to the railroad. LaGrange became a regular suburban service stop in 1869 and by 1895 it was said to be the largest of all of the towns between Chicago and Aurora and was served by 40 suburban trains daily. The growth of the community convinced the railroad to open two depots in LaGrange. The original depot in town, located on Fifth Avenue which was renamed LaGrange Road in 1937, was replaced first in 1890, and again in 1925, by the current structure. The year 1901 saw the erection of the current Stone Avenue depot, a half mile west of LaGrange Road.

(Above) On March 30, 1953, a Class O-5A leads a westbound manifest across the Burlington's bridge over the tracks of the Indiana Harbor Belt and in a moment will be rumbling over Ogden Avenue. In a matter of minutes the crossing gates will lower and the Northern will be rattling across LaGrange Road. *(Don Ball collection)*

(Opposite page, both) On a beautiful clear fall day, Ray Buhrmaster was trackside in LaGrange to photograph two of the Burlington's 4-8-4 steam locomotives which were working east with tonnage. O-5A #5634, a 1940 West Burlington product, is on track 3 and is the first to arrive. Is that a hotbox generating that smoke about five cars back? A few minutes later, O-5 #5605, following on the markers of #5634 and also on track 3, rolls by bound for Cicero. The date is September 28, 1956 and the big Northerns are back in mainline service for the grain rush. *(Both - R.W. Buhrmaster)*

THE PERMANENT ADDRESS
OF THE OWNER OF THIS PROPERTY IS:

NAME

STREET

CITY

Burlington Route

SERVING WARTIME AMERICA

CHICAGO · SAN FRANCISCO
THE VISTA-DOME
California Zephyr

Having left Chicago Union Station at 3:30 p.m., Train #17, the CALIFORNIA ZEPHYR, is less than 20 minutes into its westward journey as it crosses over Odgen Avenue between Congress Park and La Grange. It is April 1958 and E-8A #9966 and a second E-8A have the honor of piloting the CZ to its morning arrival in Denver. *(George Speir)*

Soon to complete its three day voyage from the Pacific Northwest, the eastbound MAINSTREETER, scheduled as First Train #48, has completed a conditional stop and is accelerating away from LaGrange behind E-9As #9985A and #9985B. The two EMD locomotives, constructed in the nearby EMD plant in McCook in December 1955, were less than three years old when this picture was taken in July 1958. *(George Speir)*

Getting
There is Fun.....
VIA BURLINGTON

(Above) Built at West Burlington in September 1936, #5608 was the first of the Burlington's home-built Northerns and the first Class O-5A locomotive. With the boilers furnished by Baldwin, this second group of Burlington 4-8-4s was numbered #5608-#5620. Photographed in October 1956, #5608 leads eastbound tonnage through LaGrange on track 3. *(R. W. Buhrmaster)*

(Left) Only two of the steam boiler-equipped GP-7s were outfitted with cab signals which would allow them to operate on the busy Chicago to Aurora triple track mainline. One of the two so equipped is #244, seen here in March 1961, on the point of eastbound Train #2, the all-stops local between Galesburg and Chicago. The cab signal equipment is visible on the short walkway in front of the engineer's window. Train #2's normal consist of baggage car and two coaches has been augmented this day by one of the 6100-series coaches that had been assigned to the suburban service pool since 1950. *(George Speir)*

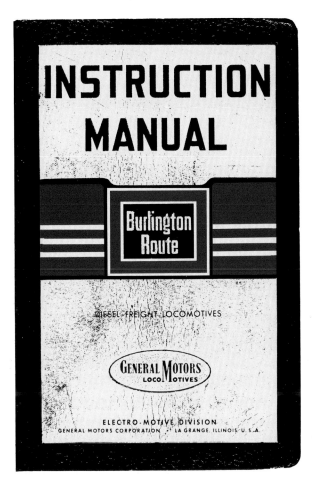

Western Springs

Located between Ogden Avenue and Plainfield Road, both formerly old plank roads for traders, trappers and stage coaches, Western Springs began in the early 1800s as a community of Quaker farmers. In 1864, the citizens persuaded the Burlington to make Western Springs a regular stop. The original depot burned and was replaced by a new structure in 1890. Western Springs continues to be a suburban service stop to this day.

(Below) The Burlington, needing additional locomotives to move wartime tonnage, received permission in 1943 from the War Production Board to acquire its first diesel freight locomotives. In early 1944 the Electro-Motive Division of General Motors began delivering 16 four-unit 5400 hp FT diesel freight locomotives to the Burlington. Fourteen year old, four-unit #110A-D is rolling through Western Springs with a westbound manifest in April 1958.
(George Speir)

(Above) On a beautiful day in June 1959, CB&Q F-3A #130A, with the passenger-style pilot intact, and three mates have westbound tonnage well in hand as they roar through Western Springs on center iron. *(George Speir)*

(Below) When the Burlington was looking for a diesel to replace the venerable M-4 2-10-4s that had proven so durable in the southern Illinois coal fields and the hill country of Nebraska, EMD responded in 1953 with the 1,500 hp SD-7 and in 1954 with the 1,750 hp SD-9. The Burlington acquired 25 of the SD-7s in 1953 (#300-324) and 50 of the SD-9s during 1954-1955 (#325-374). A large number of these work horses could be found in mainline service between Chicago and Galesburg, but today SD-7 #319 and SD-9 #346 are in command of tonnage headed for Savanna. *(George Speir)*

MAY-OCTOBER, 1957

Burlington Route

SYSTEM
TIME TABLE

Way of the Zephyrs
AND VISTA-DOMES

In 1952 the Burlington acquired seven additional Budd-built stainless steel sleeping cars and one dining car, built to the specifications used when the CALIFORNIA ZEPHYR cars were constructed in 1948. These additional cars would allow the railroad to better utilize the CZ equipment and at the same time allow the extra sleepers to be assigned to the overnight Chicago-Omaha-Lincoln train, the AK-SAR-BEN ZEPHYR. These lightweight sleepers and diner would replace older steel heavyweight cars which had held those assignments for many years. Train #30, the eastbound AK-SAR-BEN ZEPHYR, is sprinting through Western Springs in this April 1958 photo. With E-7A #9930A, a 1947 EMD product on the point, the consist of Train #30 this day includes a Louisville & Nashville heavyweight baggage, two of the Burlington's lightweight baggage cars built at the railroad's shops at Havelock, Nebraska, pre-war Budd chair cars and the CZ compatible sleepers and dome-observation. *(George Speir)*

Located 17.7 miles from the bumpers of Chicago Union Station, West Hinsdale was one of the smaller depots on the Chicago-Aurora mainline. Never as busy as some of the larger communities, it did not warrant the larger style depot found at LaGrange, Hinsdale or Naperville.

(Above) All of the O-5s were rebuilt to O-5A specifications by 1942 and the Northerns were commonly found on the Chicago-Aurora mainline, right up to the end of active steam service. On October 23, 1955, West Burlington-built O-5A #5633 charges west with a freight pulling a large block of empty reefers, many of which were bound for the meat packers in Ottumwa, St. Joseph and Omaha. *(R.W. Buhrmaster)*

Freight Trains—Westward (Information Only)

CHICAGO AND AURORA DIVISIONS.   TIME TABLE No. 29.   EFFECTIVE SEPTEMBER 25, 1949.

STATIONS	Daily Ex. Sunday Illinois Mdse.	Tuesday Thursday Saturday Way Frt.	Daily Omaha and Denver Freight	Daily Chgo. Denver Mdse.	Daily Galesburg Dead Frt.	Daily Ex. Sunday Burlington Mdse.	Daily Galesburg Time Frt.	Daily Ex. Sunday Omaha and Denver Mdse.	Daily Ex. Saturday Tri-City Mdse.	Daily Kansas City Mdse.	Daily St. Paul Mdse.	Daily Ex. Sunday Rockford and Savanna Mdse.	Daily St. Paul Mdse.	Daily Ex. Saturday Streator Mdse.
	75A	95	67	C.D.	79	73	73A	61	69	75	97	83	81	85
	A.M.			A.M.	A.M.	P.M.	P.M.		P.M.	P.M.	P.M	A.M.	P.M.	P.M.
.....CLYDE.....	L12·30			L 9·00	L11·00	L 1·30	L 7·00	L10·00	L 8·00	L 9·00	L10·00	L10·45	L10·15	L 9·30
.....EOLA.....							L 9·00		9·40					
.....MONTGOMERY.....														A12·45 A.M.
.....MENDOTA.....	5·30	A.M. L 7·25						A11·30 P.M.						
.....GALESBURG.....	A 9·30 A.M.	A 3·25 P.M.	A 2·00 P.M.	A 3·30 P.M.	A 9·30 A.M.	A 1·45 A.M.	A 3·00 A.M.	A 2·00 A.M.		A 1·30 A.M.				
.....SAVANNA.....											A 4·00 P.M.	A 5·30 A.M.	A 4·00 A.M.	

(Right) Originally constructed in 1874, the diminutive depot at West Hinsdale, originally named Stough, at one time had living quarters upstair for the agent and his family. The structure changed very little over the years and is shown here in company-standard mineral red paint with dark green trim. *(Bernard Corbin, Corbin/Wagner collection)*

(Below) With the sun setting and with the dinkie rush over for the evening, the Burlington's East End Dispatcher located in Freight House 9 at Cicero has cleared a freight with F-3A #128D on the point to head west. Beginning in 1958, the railroad's structures would have their mineral red paint replaced by a new coat of white. In this photo taken in November 1963, the quaint depot at West Hinsdale has already been repainted. *(Bob Bullermann)*

Clarendon Hills

(Top) Located 18.2 miles from Chicago Union Station and one half mile west of West Hinsdale, Clarendon Hills is another of the smaller towns on the Chicago-Aurora mainline. On April 12, 1958, F-3A #118A leads three other F units and a GP-7 westbound on Track 1 past the Clarendon Hills depot. As part of the first order of Burlington F-3s delivered in 1947, Phase II F-3 #118A was part of a four-unit set connected by drawbars. As delivered they sported high fan shrouds, a single high headlight, reflectorized numberboards beneath the headlight, two portholes with screening covering the four square vent openings between the portholes, passenger-style straight pilots and coupler covers. When this photo was taken, the lower nose door headlight had been installed and the drawbar between the B units had been replaced by couplers. Beginning in 1951, the drawbars were replaced with couplers, allowing the units to be operated independently. Although the F-units had always had an assigned suffix, these did not appear until the couplers were installed. Consequently, the reflectorized numberboards were removed and replaced by painted numbers between the headlights. *(Don Ball collection)*

Westmont

(Bottom) In May 1950 the Burlington purchased ten F-7A and three F-7B locomotives from EMD. At the time of their delivery, the Q broke up the last two four unit F-3 sets and reassembled an F-7A with a F-3B and F-3A and formed four three-unit sets numbered #163-166. The last of this group, #166, is seen here westbound through Westmont in this 1954 picture. The three unit A/B/A sets served well and would not be split up until the early 1960s. *(Bernard Corbin, Corbin/Wagner collection)*

1 9 5 5

Everywhere West

Annual Report

CHICAGO, BURLINGTON & QUINCY RAILROAD COMPANY

Burlington
Route

Lisle

Lisle, 24.4 miles from Chicago Union Station, is best known by photographers for the curve that begins about 1.4 miles west of the depot and for the Yender Road overpass located at mile post 26. This high vantage point was a favorite spot for watching the Chicago-Aurora mainline traffic.

(Above) Blasting underneath the Yender Road overpass, F-2A #158 leads its three-unit lashup east on Track 3 on a perfect day in September 1960. When EMD delivered ten F-2As to the Burlington in July 1946, they were assembled with an FT-A and FT-B to form an F-2A/FT-B/FT-A combination that resulted in a 4,050 hp locomotive set. Semi-permanently coupled together with drawbars, these units would also stay together into the 1960s and saw extensive usage on the Chicago-Twin Cities line. *(George Speir)*

Naperville

On a cold day in December 1953, Class O-1A #4984 rolls a block of emtpy reefers west through Naperville. Built by Baldwin in 1923 and assigned to the Galesburg Division, it would be retired four months after this photo was taken. *(Joe Collias)*

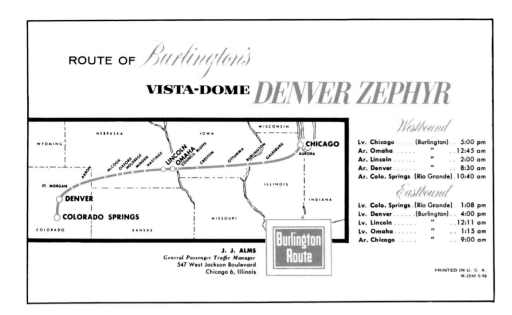

ROUTE OF *Burlington's*

VISTA-DOME DENVER ZEPHYR

Westbound

Lv. Chicago	....	(Burlington) ..	5:00 pm
Ar. Omaha	......	"	..12:45 am
Ar. Lincoln	......	"	.. 2:00 am
Ar. Denver	......	"	.. 8:30 am
Ar. Colo. Springs	.(Rio Grande).	10:40 am

Eastbound

Lv. Colo. Springs	.(Rio Grande)	1:08 pm
Lv. Denver	.....	.(Burlington)..	4:00 pm
Lv. Lincoln	......	"	..12:11 am
Lv. Omaha	......	"	.. 1:15 am
Ar. Chicago	.....	"	.. 9:00 am

J. J. ALMS
General Passenger Traffic Manager
547 West Jackson Boulevard
Chicago 6, Illinois

Burlington
Route

PRINTED IN U. S. A.
K-25M-5-59

In 1956, the Burlington completely re-equipped its overnight Chicago-Denver passenger train, the DENVER ZEPHYR, with new Budd-built stainless steel coaches, diner, sleepers and dome cars. The new Vista-Dome DENVER ZEPHYR, Train #1, left Chicago Union Station at 5:00 p.m. for an overnight sprint to Denver where it would arrive at 8:30 the next morning.

THE CHUCK WAGON DZ

(Below) This flagship of the ZEPHYR fleet would normally be pulled by the Burlington's EMD E-9 2,400 hp locomotives, the newest and most powerful passenger engines on the roster. CB&Q E-9A #9995, built by EMD in August 1954, is less than four years old when photographed in July 1958 with westbound Train #1, with three additional E-units and an 18 car consist. The location is the Naperville curve, just a mile east of the depot. *(George Speir)*

(Above) CB&Q #209, one of the Phase 1 GP-7s built in 1951, is seen eastbound on track 1 with the East End Way Freight. Scheduled out of Eola early in the morning, it would work east to Congress Park where it would set out cars for the Indiana Harbor Belt return to Eola and then tie up. *(Chuck Zeiler)*

(Below) Bound for the yard at Cicero, F-3A #116D and two mates lead a manifest through Naperville. *(Chuck Zeiler)*

Eola Yard

Located 33 miles from Chicago Union Station, and just east of Aurora, is Eola Yard. With its small yard, engine facility and reclamation plant, Eola was a center of mainline freight and way freight activity. Eola would dispatch way freights to work the mainlines east to Congress Park, west to Earlville and northwest to Oregon. Additional way freights would work the branches south to Ottawa and Streator, west to Rock Falls, north to West Chicago and north to Mooseheart and West Batavia. At the east end of the yard was the interchange with the Elgin, Joliet & Eastern.

(Above) The Burlington acquired its first batch of NW-2 switchers from EMD during 1940 and 1941. Ordering 17 of the 1,000 hp units, the CB&Q would number them #9203-9219. On August 5, 1958, NW-2 #9216, with wood waycar #13926, is resting between assignments near the coaling tower at Eola. Anywhere from 3 to 5 NW-2s could usually be found working in and around Eola. Cabooses on the Burlington were called waycars, and this one, built by the Aurora shops in July, 1914 and classified as an NE-7, was assigned to Eola for way freight service. To the left of the waycar in the distance is the Eola turntable and roundhouse. The coaling tower, with a 150 ton capacity, was erected in 1914. *(Bernard Corbin, Corbin/Wagner collection)*

(Left) Built by Baldwin twenty-five years earlier, the first of the Burlington's Northerns, •5600, was on the ready track at the Eola roundhouse on July 3, 1955. Outfitted with a Mars light and cab signal equipment in April 1953, it was assigned to the Galesburg Division and used in mainline freight service until its fires would finally be dropped near the end of 1956.
(Max Zimmerlein collection)

(Below) On October 1, 1964, CB&Q #121A and a companion B-unit lead a Galesburg-bound freight through the curve between mileposts 32 and 33, which is just east of the EJ&E overpass at Eola. Built in November 1947 as a Phase II F-3A, #121D would last until August 1966 when it would be traded in on a new U28C from General Electric. *(Chuck Zeiler)*

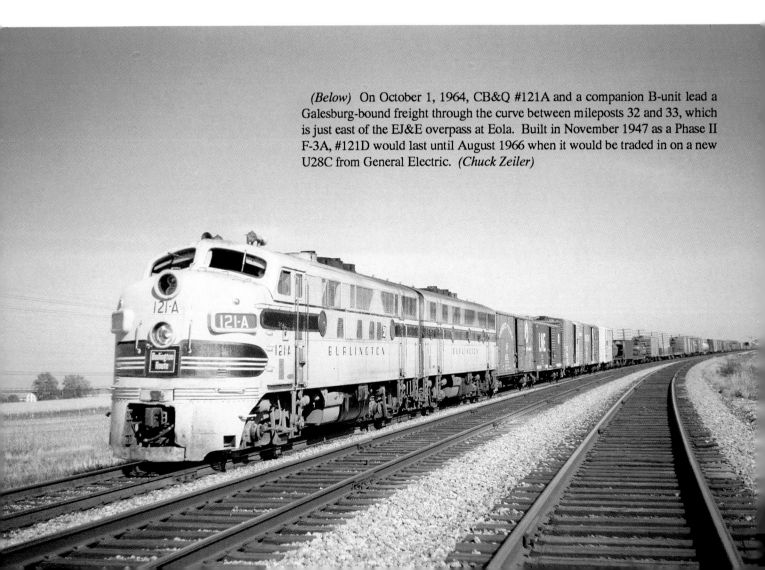

(Top) This scene, looking west from the Vaughn Road overpass, provides an overall view of the Burlington's reclamation facility. The railroad would send all of its old equipment to Eola, salvage as many usable parts as possible and cut up the rest for scrap. Here we can see the facility as it looked in the early 1960s; there are a number of composite boxcars in the process of being cut up. The stock cars on the first yard track are also destined for the plant. *(Bob Bullermann)*

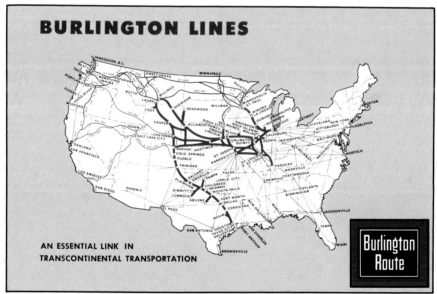

BURLINGTON LINES

AN ESSENTIAL LINK IN
TRANSCONTINENTAL TRANSPORTATION

Burlington Route

(Bottom) Turning to the east, the view from the Vaughn Road overpass reveals a string of old wood waycars bound for the reclamation plant. The old wood waycars, many fifty and sixty years old, were undoubtedly declared excess when new steel waycars delivered during 1960-1964 were put into service. The Eola interlocking tower can be seen above the last of the waycars. In the distance is the EJ&E overpass. *(Bob Bullermann)*

Aurora

Beginning as a stage coach transfer in the 1830s, Aurora would forever be impacted by the incorporation in 1849 of the Aurora Branch Railroad. Chartered to build a twelve mile line from Aurora and Batavia to Turner Junction (now West Chicago) where it connected with the Galena & Chicago Union, the little road began operations in 1850. The road was renamed in 1857 to the Chicago & Aurora, and subsequently on February 14, 1855 to the Chicago, Burlington and Quincy Railroad Company. The Galena & Chicago Union gave notice to the Q in 1857 that it would be terminating the trackage rights agreement that had provided the little railroad access from Aurora to Chicago. Surveys showed that a direct line between Aurora and Chicago would be six miles shorter than the former route and could be built for $800,000. Construction began in 1862 and the new line began service in May 1864. Aurora, the birthplace of the Burlington, would grow and prosper with the railroad. A large warehouse facility, along with a cut stone roundhouse, would be joined by the company's passenger car shop. It would become the western terminus of suburban service and the spot where the mainline to Minneapolis/St. Paul would diverge from the Chicago-Galesburg main.

Burlington
Route

Your
**COMMUTATION
TICKET**

(Below) Situated between the freight yard at Eola and downtown Aurora, Hill Yard was the home of the railroad's general warehouse, passenger car shops and suburban service layover facility. In this May 1964 photo, the number of gallery cars and heavyweight suburban service cars indicates that this was shot on a weekend when most of the suburban fleet was in Aurora, readying themselves for the Monday morning rush hour. The general warehouse is seen beyond the suburban cars, while the triple track mainline is on the hill to the left. *(G. Allbach)*

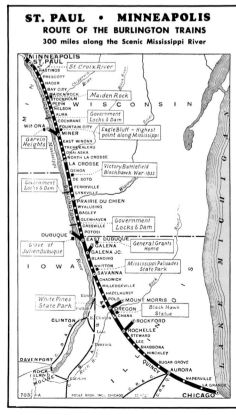

The Burlington introduced ZEPHYR service between Chicago and Minneapolis/St. Paul in April 1935. The response was so overwhelming that the original equipment was replaced in 1936 by TWIN ZEPHYRS #9904 and 9905. These seven-car trainsets could carry 203 revenue passengers, compared with the earlier ZEPHYR's #9901 and 9902, which could accomodate only 88 passengers. The seven car TWIN ZEPHYRS would make the daily roundtrip between the Windy City and the Twin Cities until December 1947 when the Burlington introduced the Vista-Dome TWIN CITIES ZEPHYR. Each of the two new trains consisted of a baggage-lounge car, 4 Vista-Dome coaches, a 48-seat diner and a Vista-Dome parlor observation.

(Both) With E-7A #9926A and two additional E-7s providing 6,000 horsepower, Train #23, the AFTERNOON ZEPHYR, rolls westward on the mainline curve above Hill Yard in Aurora. It is July 1958 and Train #23, with a ten car consist, is headed for its early evening date with the Q's Mississippi River Scenic Line. Scheduled out of Aurora at 4:49 p.m., the AFTERNOON ZEPHYR will arrive in Savanna at 6:20 p.m. where the Burlington's tracks turn north and run parallel to the Mississippi to the Twin Cities. *(Both- George Speir)*

(Top) The Burlington's roster of EMD SW-1 switchers, #9136-9153, were delivered in three groups beginning in June 1939, with the last units, #9148-9153, arriving in February 1941. The last locomotive, #9153, was used at Aurora as the depot, coach yard and shop engine from shortly after its purchase until the merger in 1970. This engine replaced the Class O-1 2-8-2s that had been assigned as the depot engines in Aurora. It is seen here in 1965 awaiting its next orders. (G. Allbach)

"Ridin' high, wide and handsome!"

Glass-enclosed observation dome on a BURLINGTON ZEPHYR

Glass-enclosed observation dome cars like the above are now in service on the Burlington's Twin Cities Zephyrs, and soon will be running on the new California Zephyrs. These fast, luxurious streamline Zephyrs, as well as most other Burlington main line trains, are powered by General Motors Diesel locomotives. Other principal Burlington trains so powered include:— the Denver, Nebraska, Texas, Pioneer, Mark Twain, Sam Houston, and Silver Streak Zephyrs, and the Zephyr-Rocket.

(Bottom) When #9153 was in for routine maintenance, one of the NW-2s would normally fill in as the depot switcher. On June 15, 1957, NW-2 #9205, a February 1941 EMD product, is moving past the Railway Express building with one of the suburban service generator cars. To the left of the switcher cab is one of the Burlington's baggage-express cars built from a troop kitchen car. The railroad had purchased 300 surplus troop kitchens after World War II and sent them to the railroad's car shops at Havelock, Nebraska where they were modified for express service. Since they came from the U.S. Army, the cars were affectionately known as "Geeps." (M. Spoor collection)

(Top) An eastbound CALIFORNIA ZEPHYR, with dome-observation *Silver Sky* on the rear, is at the Aurora depot in this November 1964 photo. When Train #18 pulls out of the depot, it has only 38 miles left on its 2,537 mile run from Oakland, California. *(Chuck Zeiler)*

(Center) In this May 1961 photo, Train #10, the eastbound DENVER ZEPHYR, with E-9A #9985A on the point, prepares to stop at the Aurora depot, while the fireman on Train #21, the MORNING ZEPHYR, impatiently waits for the conductor's signal. *(Mike Gleason)*

(Bottom) F-3A #129A leads a Cicero-bound freight through the Aurora depot on June 26, 1965. This 1948 EMD product would be traded in on a new GP-40 in 18 months. *(Chuck Zeiler)*

The Chicago & Iowa

In 1869 the Illinois Legislature approved a Special Act which incorporated a new railroad called the Chicago and Iowa Railroad Company which was chartered to build a line from Chicago to a crossing of the Rock River at, or near, the town of Oregon and then to the Mississippi River at Savanna. Having worked out an arrangement with the CB&Q

to carry its traffic east of Aurora, the C&I began laying track west towards Rochelle in 1870, reaching that town in January, 1871. Oregon was reached in April of 1871, and the line was extended an additional 18 miles to Forreston in January 1872 where the C&I connected with the Illinois Central. In June 1899, the C&I was merged into the CB&Q, but to this day the dispatchers still refer to this line as the "C&I."

(Opposite page, top) F-3A #123A leads westbound freight #97 through the curve at milepost 82, just one mile east of Rochelle. It is July 24, 1960 and the F-unit still has its coupler cover. *(Barry Carlson)*

(Opposite page, bottom) In September 1958, CB&Q F-3A #129A, an F-3B, FT-B and an FT-A were rolling Train #97 under the two track coaling tower at milepost 82. The Burlington purchased a large number of 100,000 gallon capacity steel water tanks from Chicago Bridge and Iron Works, one of which is seen here in company-standard mineral red paint. These water tanks were used throughout the system. *(Barry Carlson)*

The first large town on the C&I west of Aurora is Rochelle. Founded in 1853, the town was originally called Lane after the founder, R.P. Lane. The State Legislature changed the name to Rochelle in 1866. Because of the abundance of excellent farm land the town prospered. The arrival of two railroads, the C&I and the Chicago & Northwestern, provided the stimulus for the development of several commercial industries. Each railroad had its own depot and the tracks would cross at grade just west of the town's business district.

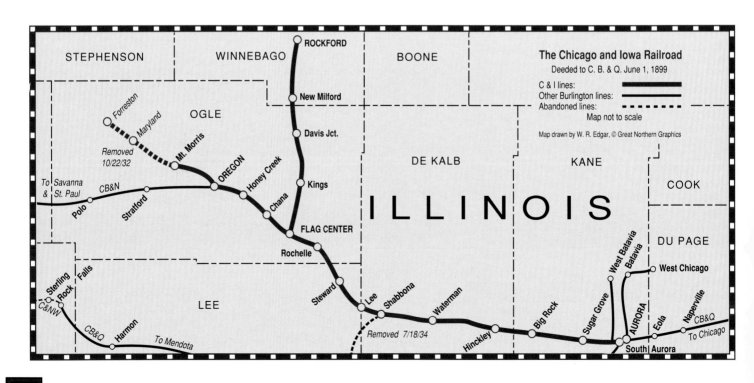

America's Distinctive Trains

(Opposite page, top) One of the150-series three F-unit lashups clatters across the C&NW diamond in this 1955 photo. The train is #97, the daily St. Paul Merchandise, which left Cicero at 11:00 a.m. FT-A #159 is scheduled to have #97 across the C&I and in the yard at Savanna by 2:15 p.m. *(Barry Carlson)*

(Opposite page, bottom) Later on the same day, Barry Carlson caught the westbound EMPIRE BUILDER, Train #49, storming through Rochelle. The Burlington's first E-8A, #9937B, is in command this day and will momentarily be crossing the C&NW diamond. The second unit is one of the two EA-B units built in 1936 for the articulated DENVER ZEPHYR. After the arrival of the E-7s and E-8s in the late 1940s and early 1950s, the EA-Bs were normally found spliced between two of the larger EMD locomotives. Beginning in 1953, "Diesel Passenger Power Pool #3" called for two 2,250 hp E-8As and one 1,200 hp EA-B to be assigned to the EMPIRE BUILDER. *(Barry Carlson)*

(Below) The Great Northern introduced dome coaches to the EMPIRE BUILDER on May 29, 1955. Each train received three of these Budd-built cars that provided for 60 coach seats and 24 dome seats which were called "Great Domes" by the Great Northern. They were followed by the full-length dome lounge cars, which went into service in October 1955. The Great Northern called these cars "Great Dome Lounges" and they were reserved for sleeping car passengers. Here, in this photo taken in November 1955, the westbound EMPIRE BUILDER, complete with 3 E-units, 3 Great Domes and a Great Dome Lounge, rolls across the fill between mileposts 91 and 92, eight miles west of Rochelle. *(M. Spoor collection)*

Oregon

In April 1871, the C&I reached the east bank of the Rock River near the small town of Oregon . The covered bridge across the Rock River was completed by October of that year, which allowed the first trains to arrive just south of town at the new wood frame depot. As had been the case in Rochelle, Oregon's economy flourished with the arrival of the railroad. A number of businesses opened along the western bank of the Rock River and the C&I built a spur to run north into town to serve them. In the 1920s a fire badly damaged the wood depot and a new brick and stucco structure was erected as a replacement. The old wood depot was moved a few hundred feet to the west, repaired and converted into the freight house which lasted into the 1960s. The 1920s depot still stands and is now the property of the Ogle County Historical Society.

(Opposite page, top) On Independence Day 1958, another three-unit F-2A/FT-B/FT-A combination, this time #154ABC, moves past the Oregon depot with Train #82, eastbound from Savanna and bound for Eola and Cicero. For many years there was a small park just east of the cars in the depot's parking lot where the station agent maintained a flower garden. Water for the park and garden came from one of those Chicago Bridge and Iron steel water tanks which was just a few feet further east. The old wood freight house can barely be seen between #154 and the depot. *(Barry Carlson)*

(Opposite page, bottom) On a glorious July day in 1958, a number of railfans have gathered in Oregon to watch O-5A #5618 on the point of an eastbound steam excursion. Before the steam train can proceed east of Oregon, Train #97, with F-3A #136D in the lead, must cross the Rock River bridge and make the siding at Oregon. Moving cautiously through the siding and past the stockpens on the right, the crew on #97 is mindful of railfans roaming at will through the small yard. The trainman from the steam excursion will perform the requisite inspection of #97 as it rolls by. *(Russ Porter, M. Spoor collection)*

(Right) In 1932, the line to Forreston was abandoned back to Mt. Morris, just 8 miles from Oregon. The short branch was left intact because of the amount of traffic generated by the businesses in Mt. Morris, chiefly a company called Kable Printing Company. The large number of shippers in Oregon and Mt. Morris required that the railroad have a permanent switcher based in Oregon. This was normally handled by an NW-2 based in Oregon. In July 1960, NW-2 #9207 is on the station track just east of the depot. *(M. Spoor collection)*

Chicago, Burlington & Northern

Between 1872 and 1880, the CB&Q gained virtual control over the C&I, and while the line to Forreston was put in service in 1872, management of the CB&Q wanted to push towards the Mississippi and a shorter route to Savanna and hence to the Twin Cities. On October 1, 1881, Charles E. Perkins was elected President of the CB&Q and within a year he had taken the inital steps to build a railroad along the eastern bank of the Mississippi. Perkins, having the foresight to see the enormous growth potential of the Pacific Northwest that would materialize when the Northern Pacific was completed in 1883, wanted the CB&Q to be positioned to take advantage of the opportunity. Accordingly, a new company, the Chicago, Burlington and Northern Railroad Company was incorporated on November 14, 1883, and its directors authorized a full-fledged survey in December 1883. In 1884, the CB&N decided to extend west from Oregon to Savanna and then build 288 miles along the east bank of the Mississippi, resulting in a Chicago-St. Paul route only 435 miles long. While this would be only 25 miles longer than the competing C&NW and Milwaukee Road, it would have better grades than the competition. Construction began in late 1885, with the line finished in August, 1886. A comprehensive corporate consolidation resulted in both the C&I and the CB&N being deeded to the CB&Q on June 1, 1899.

White Pines State Park

Located between the towns of Polo and Carter, or mileposts 112 and 116, White Pines State Park has been a favorite destination for picnickers, campers and railfans. On September 19, 1954, Barry Carlson was at White Pines State Park to record the parade of Chicago-Pacific Northwest passenger trains that the Burlington had responsibility for between Chicago and the Twin Cities.

(Left) Scheduled out of Savanna at 12:25 p.m., Train #44, the eastbound EMPIRE BUILDER, is on the advertised and will meet the westbound NORTH COAST LIMITED between Rochelle and Aurora. With E-8A #9945A on the point, it is seen here on the curve inside the park at milepost 113.5. *(Barry Carlson)*

(Above) E-8A #9975 and an E-5A, having met Train #44 east of Rochelle, have the westbound NORTH COAST LIMITED well in hand on its run from Chicago to St. Paul and are due in Savanna at 1:45 p.m. All but the last two cars wear the Northern Pacific's Raymond Loewy-inspired two-tone green paint scheme adopted in 1952. Included in the consist of #25 this day are two of the new Budd-built Vista-Dome coaches, which were put into service on the NCL in July and August of 1954. With the Vista-Dome sleepers still two months away, the two sleepers on the end of the train, still wearing their original two-tone green paint scheme, will undoubtedly be shopped for repainting as soon as the Vista-Dome sleepers are placed in service. *(Barry Carlson)*

(Right) The westbound EMPIRE BUILDER, Train #49, is rolling through the park with its then standard motive power combination of an E-8/EA-B/E-8A. Train #49, with CB&Q E-8A #9967 that is only 25 months old, was scheduled out of Aurora at 1:36 p.m. and is due in Savanna at 3:15 p.m., 107.8 miles in 99 minutes. *(Barry Carlson)*

(Top) Eight miles east of Savanna, the Burlington's right-of-way goes through a shallow cut at milepost 134.3, allowing Illinois Highway 78 to pass overhead. On this day in September 1958, the westbound NORTH COAST LIMITED, led by E-9A #9988B, passes under the overpass. The first car is a Budd-built sleeper being deadheaded to the Twin Cities. The rest of the train has been repainted in the Northern Pacific's Raymond Loewy-inspired two-tone green scheme adopted in 1952. In the consist of #25 this day are two Vista-Domes coaches and two Vista-Dome sleepers which were introduced to the NCL four years earlier. *(Barry Carlson)*

(Bottom) On Independence Day 1960, the Burlington sponsored a steam fantrip from Chicago over the C&I using Northern #5632. A problem developed when the steam engine broke an eccentric rod near White Pines State Park. Two E-units were summoned from Aurora to rescue the stranded train. E-8A #9972 and an E-7A are seen here with the fantrip on the eastbound part of the trip near East Dubuque. *(Barry Carlson)*

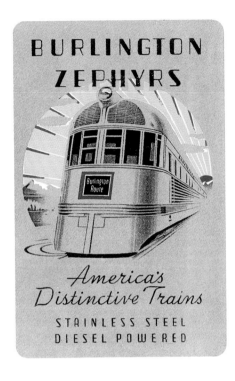

BURLINGTON
ZEPHYRS

America's
Distinctive Trains

STAINLESS STEEL
DIESEL POWERED

La Crosse

The La Crosse and Milwaukee Railroad, a predecessor of the Milwaukee Road, was the first railroad to reach La Crosse, arriving there in 1857. Twenty one years later, in 1876, the tracks of the Green Bay & Minnesota Railroad, later to be known as the Green Bay & Western, came into La Crosse. The C&NW, not wanting to be left out of the La Crosse market, entered into a trackage agreement with the GB&M in 1873 which allowed the C&NW to use GB&M iron to enter La Crosse. The last railroad to reach La Crossse was the CB&N, arriving there in 1886.

La Crosse welcomed the added rail competitor, granting permission to the CB&N to run down the middle of 2nd Street to get to the central business area. While the CB&N wanted the line through town to get passenger business, it was slow and congested, so in 1887 it built a freight line east of town and near the base of the bluffs to the east. Since the lines of all four railroads crossed north of the downtown area, this location in North La Crosse became known as Grand Crossing. Because of the connections with the other lines and the availability of land, the CB&N elected North La Crosse as the site of the division headquarters, yard and and shop facilities.

(Below) Built in 1929-1930, the CB&Q depot in North La Crosse replaced an old wooden structure built there in 1888 and housed the railroad's division offices which were moved from the original CB&N depot located at 2nd & Pearl Street. The original CB&N station was torn down and replaced by a smaller and more modern depot on the same location. The North La Crosse depot was an all-brick structure which also housed the division's superintendent and dispatchers. It is seen here in July 1964. *(Bob Bullermann)*

Beginning in 1940, all CB&Q passenger trains stopped at the new South Side depot built at the east end of Main Street. Service to the old 1929 depot at 2nd and Pearl Street was discontinued, with the result being that the Burlington eliminated thirty-one street crossings and street running in downtown La Crosse. Additionally, 15-20 minutes were removed from the Chicago-Minneapolis schedules.

THE MISSISSIPPI RIVER *Scenic Line*

Burlington Route

Route of the TWIN ZEPHYRS

(Top) Train #49, the northbound EMPIRE BUILDER, is at the La Crosse depot in this 1954 photo. E-8A #9943B will have the 15 car mid-century EMPIRE BUILDER out on the advertised 5:21 p.m. and in St. Paul at 7:45 p.m. The equipment on #49 was only three years old, having been delivered in 1951 when the Great Northern completely re-equipped its flagship train. *(M. Spoor collection)*

(Bottom) About to roll to a stop at the South Side depot, Burlington Train #24, the AFTERNOON ZEPHYR, is led by an E-5A and E-5B. The consist today is missing the normal round-ended dome-observation and in its place appears to be one of the pre-World War II dining-par-lor-observation cars. A pre-war flattop coach has been spliced in between the third and fourth Vista-Domes. The La Crosse Country Club is to the right, while Grandad Bluff projects above the ZEPHYR.
(M. Spoor collection)

Minneapolis - St. Paul

(Above) The MORNING ZEPHYR rolls past Daytons Bluff and in a moment will pass Hoffman Avenue tower which is just minutes away from St. Paul Union Depot, where #21 is scheduled to arrive at 2:30 p.m. It is January 12, 1958 and one of the four Vista-Domes has been replaced by a post-war flattop chair car. The E-5A /E-5B tandem will have Train #21 in Minneapolis at 3:00 p.m. where it will be turned and serviced for its 3:30 p.m. departure as Train #22, the AFTERNOON ZEPHYR. It will end up in Chicago, back where it started the day, at 10:15 p.m after completing the 874 mile roundtrip between Chicago and the Twin Cities. *(M. Spoor collection)*

(Right) Between St. Paul Union Station and the Great Northern's Passenger Station in Minneapolis, the Burlington operated over trackage rights obtained from the Great Northern. North of the GN Station was the small CB&Q Coach Yard which included a small engine servicing facility. E-8A #9948A and one of the EA-Bs are being serviced in this photo taken in May 1955.
(Russ Porter, M. Spoor collection)

Aurora - Galesburg Mainline

On October 20, 1853 the Chicago and Aurora Railroad completed construction of 45 miles of trackage from Aurora to Mendota. The Central Military Tract Railroad, on friendly enough terms with management of the C&A that the latter would advance funds to the Central Military Tract, finished construction of the 79.5 miles between Mendota and Galesburg on December 7, 1854. With vision and foresight, C&A President James F. Joy persuaded the Illinois Legislature to permit the C&A to adopt the name *The Chicago, Burlington And Quincy Railroad Company*. On July 9, 1856, the stockholders of the CB&Q and the Central Military Tract agreed to merge under the title *The Chicago, Burlington & Quincy Rail Road Company*. While the consolidated company operated a line from from Aurora to Galesburg, it would not be until 1864 that, through acquisitions, mergers and name changes, the CB&Q would reach all of the cities in its corporate name. Beginning in 1867, steel rail started replacing iron, and in 1872 management recognized that traffic warranted the double-tracking of the mainline between Aurora and Mendota. This was completed between the two cities in 1872. The project was completed from Mendota to Galesburg in 1886.

Aurora to Galesburg

Distance from Aurora	STATIONS
	........AURORA........
2.22	........MONTGOMERY........
7.72	........BRISTOL........
13.71	........PLANO........
18.10	........SANDWICH........
21.45	........SOMONAUK........
27.56	........LELAND........
34.34	........EARLVILLE........
34.59	C. & N. W. Cross'g (Interlocked)
40.30	........MERIDEN........
43.95	........MS TOWER........
44.89	........MENDOTA........
45.06	..I. C. Crossing (Interlocked)..
49.80	........CLARION........
53.65	........ARLINGTON........
57.53	........ZEARING........
60.67	........MALDEN........
66.42	........PRINCETON........
72.93	........WYANET........
78.80	........BUDA........
85.21	........NEPONSET........
93.19	........KEWANEE........
101.50	........GALVA........
101.76	C.R.I.& P. Cross'g (Interlocked)
108.93	........ALTONA........
113.01	........ONEIDA........
117.35	........WATAGA........
119.91	........BISHOP........
124.47	........GALESBURG........

Sandwich

(Below) Located 18 miles west of Aurora is the small farming community of Sandwich. Here U.S. Route 34 parallels the CB&Q main and provides numerous locations to photograph the busy double-track thoroughfare of the Burlington. On May 27, 1959, F-3A #130D leads a westbound manifest freight through town. *(M. Spoor collection)*

Somonauk

(Above) O-5A #5630, with an eastbound freight, was on the west end of Sandwich and in the process of setting out some stock cars at the stock pens when Max Zimmerlein took this photo on October 14, 1956. Only 16 years old, from all appearances it has been well maintained by the mechanical department. Unfortunately the transition to diesels will cause it to be prematurely retired at the end of the year. *(Max Zimmerlein)*

(Below) Three miles west of Sandwich is Somonauk which, like Sandwich, had a small depot, freight house and stock pens. Somonauk was different from Sandwich because it had a wooden interlocking tower and the town's distinctive water tower. O-5A #5630, complete with Mars light, seems to have this westbound empty hopper train well in hand as it passes the Somonauk water tower on October 9, 1955. *(R.W. Buhrmaster)*

Mendota

The C&A's tracks arrived in Mendota in 1853, only two years after the Illinois Central completed its line which ran north to Galena and south to Bloomington and Decatur. In 1854 a large depot to be used by both railroads was constructed and, because it had hotel facilities, it became known as the Passenger House. In 1885, a fire totally destroyed this structure but immediately afterwards an all-brick Union Depot, nearly a city block long, was constructed.

In 1870, the CB&Q acquired a small line built in the1860s that ran from Mendota west towards the Mississippi River to the town of Denrock. This line, passing through bountiful farm land, served numerous small farming communities along its route. At Denrock it connected with the Burlington's line running north out of Galesburg to Savanna. In 1922, to service the engines used on what was known as the Denrock Branch, the Burlington constructed a turntable and a seven-stall roundhouse on the east side of Mendota.

The last railroad to enter Mendota was the Milwaukee Road, arriving in 1903. It built a small depot south of the CB&Q/IC diamond, but by the 1930s the Milwaukee discontinued passenger service. The IC dropped passenger service in 1939, leaving the CB&Q as the sole owner of the Union Depot. In 1942, the Burlington, seeing no reason to maintain the large structure, demolished it and replaced it with a much smaller, one-story brick facility.

MARCH-APRIL, 1949

Burlington Route

1829 100th Anniversary *1949*

TIME TABLES

EVERYWHERE WEST

(Below) Four-unit FT #105 was nine years old when this photo was taken in 1952 from MS Tower on the east side of Mendota. With #105A in the lead, this classic FT lashup with its westbound freight is bound for Galesburg. MS Tower was responsible for handing up orders to trains eastbound out of Mendota as well as controlling the crossovers on the east side of town. MS was torn down in 1962 when the Burlington completed installation of remote control switches and crossovers in Mendota. *(Mike Gleason)*

MARCH-APRIL, 1949

Burlington
Route

1849 100th Anniversary 1949

TIME TABLES

EVERYWHERE WEST

(Above) When delivered, all of the Burlington's E-5s were given names. In this photo taken in 1953, E-5A #9913, *Silver Wings*, is piloting Train #19, the COLORADOAN, past MS Tower. Train #19 went into the timetable in December 1947 as a daytime secondary train between Chicago and Omaha. The March 1949 timetable change saw it begin operating as the COLORADOAN, now operating all the way to Denver. *(Mike Gleason)*

(Below) In addition to the 10 FT-A/FT-B/F2-A locomotives, the Burlington also acquired three F-3A/F-3B/F-3A lashups which were numbered #160-162. Rolling past MS Tower, #162 is headed west and is about to go under the large coal tower located at milepost 82. On the left is another of the steel water tanks manufactured by Chicago Bridge & Iron. *(Mike Gleason)*

63

(Above) CB&Q FTA#115A, in charge of westbound freight #67, is crossing 8th Street, while waycar #14653 is on the rear of an eastbound local freight. (Mike Gleason)

Burlington Route — **Everywhere West**

Chicago-Omaha-Lincoln

All Through Trains are Air-Conditioned
For equipment of these trains see page 7

WESTBOUND—Read Down Table No. 1 **EASTBOUND—Read Up**

33 Ex.Su.	55 Daily	5 Daily	9 Daily	7 Daily	3 Daily	15 Daily	1 Daily	17 Daily	11 Daily	19 Daily	Miles	Central Standard Time — Stations shown in *italics* indicate connections	10 Daily	18 Daily	12 Daily	6 Daily	14 Daily	30 Daily	56 Daily	4 Daily	2 Daily	32 Ex.Su.
PM	PM	PM	AM	AM	PM	PM	PM	PM	PM	AM			AM	PM	AM	PM	PM	AM	AM	AM	AM	AM
3 45	6 30	4 40	9 30	12.15	10.00	7.50	5 30	3 30	12.45	11.30	0	Lv. Chicago (Union Sta.) Ar	8.35	1.30	8.45	9 30	7.00	8.00	8 55	11.00	11.35	7.37
4 12											14	La Grange, La Grange Road										
5 00	7 16		10.16	1.01	10.46		6 04				38	Ar. Aurora, 2, 20 Lv	M7.55		A 7.57	8 40	6.13	8.09	J 8.09	J10.55	J10.54	6 37
5 13	7 20		10.21	1.11	10.48						38	Lv. Fox River Ar				8.35	6.10	7.15	J 8.06	J10.07	J10.54	6 33
5 24											46	Bristol							9 55			6 21
5 33			10.38	g 1.27							52	Plano							9 46	J10.34		6 11
5 40	J 5 28		10.45	g 1.35							56	Sandwich				8.15			9 34			6 03
5 45			10.51								59	Somonauk							9 25			5 57
5 53			10.59								66	Leland							9 15			5 48
6 02			11.09								72	Earlville, 21							9 05			5 39
6 09											78	Meriden										5 31
6 17	8 04	J 5 54	11.25	2.17	11.26						83	Mendota, 26				7.45	5.24		J 7.19	J10.03		5 25
			11.34								92	Arlington							8 31			
			11.40								96	Zearing, 27							8 22			
			11.46								99	Malden							8 15			
176 Ex.Su.	8 30	J 6 16	11.56	2.48							104	Princeton				7.11			8 08	J 9.45		177 Ex.Su.
Motor			12.05								111	Wyanet							7 56			Motor
8 50			12.14								117	Buda, 34				6.53	b 4.49		7 46			
			12.23								123	Neponset							7 33			
	J 6 43	12 40	3.38	12.15				2.34			131	Kewanee		6.33		6 36	D 4.34		J 6.24	J 9.23		3 05
10.10	9 27		12.50	4.00							139	Galva, 33				6.21	4.22		7 22	J 9.12		2 55
10.20											147	Altona, 33							7 08			2 48
10.27											151	Oneida, 33							6 54			2 41
10.39											155	Wataga, 33							6 48			
10.45	9 58	J 7 14	1 30	4.30	12.45	10 20	7 40	5 45	3.00	1.53	162	Ar. Galesburg 3, 7, 30 Lv	6.18	11.02	6.00	5 50	3.55	5.10	6 41	J 8.54		2 30
AM	PM	PM	AM	AM	PM	AM	PM	PM	AM	AM			AM	AM	AM	PM	PM	AM	AM	AM	AM	PM

(Left) Train #9 was the daily westbound except Sunday, all-stops local between Chicago and Galesburg. Burlington E-5A #9910A, *Silver Speed*, has Train #9 at the Mendota depot on the advertised at 5:14 p.m. It will arrive in Galesburg at 7:40 p.m. It is 1953 and Train #9 would be dropped from the timetable effective May 1954. (Mike Gleason)

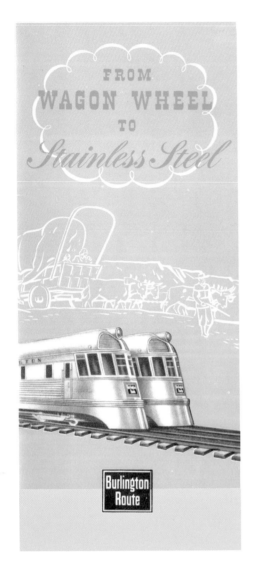

(Above) From June 1947 through February 1954, ZEPHYR #9902 ran in Chicago-Galesburg-Burlington-Hannibal service, working as Train #5 westbound and Train #2 eastbound. The schedule, designed to give passengers an afternoon to conduct business or go shopping in the Windy City, called for the train to depart Hannibal at 5:50 a.m. It would make 14 stops and would arrive in Chicago at 11:40 a.m. With business and shopping completed, #9902 would depart Chicago Union Station at 5:40 p.m. and would eventually arrive back in Hannibal at 11:25 p.m. ZEPHYR #9902 is seen in this 1953 shot at the Mendota depot loading passengers for its eastbound run to Chicago. *(Mike Gleason)*

(Below) When ZEPHYR # 9902 was in the shop for routine maintenance, or when seasonal traffic warranted, Train #2's normal ZEPHYR consist was replaced by heavyweight coaches. Steam generator-equipped GP-7s, or even an occassional Class S-4 or S-4A Hudson, would be called on to power the train. Train #2, with three 6100-series coaches, is at the Mendota depot loading a large group of passengers headed for Chicago. *(Mike Gleason)*

The M-4A 2-10-4s were rarely seen east of Galesburg, but on October 21, 1956, Ray Buhrmaster caught #6323 steaming through Mendota bound for Galesburg. It had most likely been pressed into service for the fall grain rush. *(R.W. Buhrmaster)*

Burlington Route

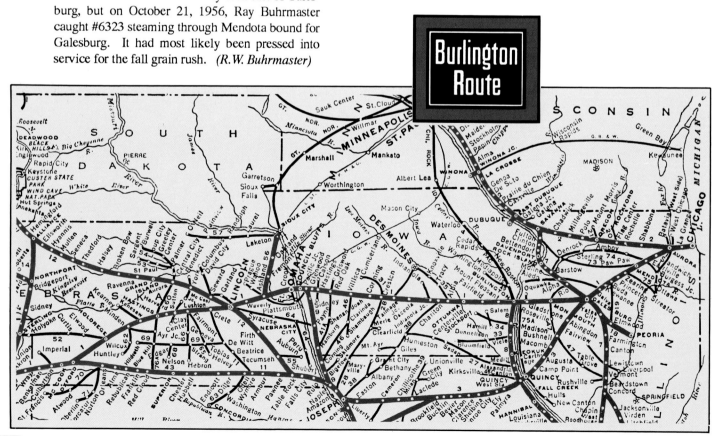

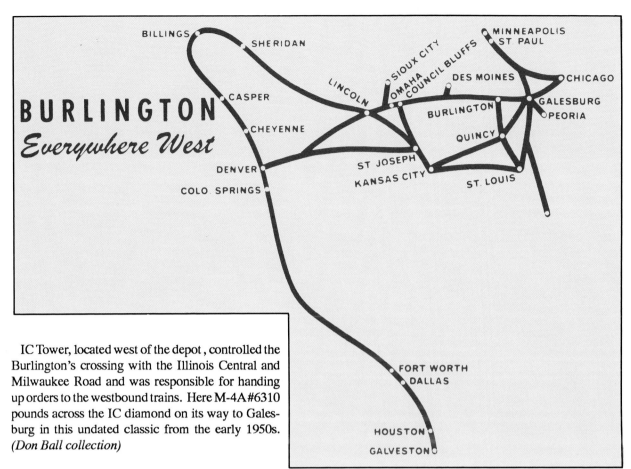

BURLINGTON
Everywhere West

IC Tower, located west of the depot, controlled the Burlington's crossing with the Illinois Central and Milwaukee Road and was responsible for handing up orders to the westbound trains. Here M-4A #6310 pounds across the IC diamond on its way to Galesburg in this undated classic from the early 1950s. *(Don Ball collection)*

When the Burlington ordered equipment from Budd for the new CALIFORNIA ZEPHYR, it also placed an order for three A/B/A sets of Phase II F-3s to power its leg of the run. Numbered #9960-9962 and delivered in October 1947, they came from EMD in the Q's passenger paint scheme of silver with black nose stripes and were the only F-units on the system to have steam generators. They also had the distinction of being the only CB&Q F-units without dynamic brakes. The choice of F-3s was unusual because, with this one exception, the Burlington relied on the EMD E-units to power its passenger trains. By 1954 the passenger F-3s would be bumped from CZ service to be used on secondary passenger trains and in 1955 they would be regeared, repainted and placed in freight service.

the California Zephyr

DAILY BETWEEN CHICAGO • DENVER • SALT LAKE CITY • SAN FRANCISCO

Diesel-Powered
for smooth, effortless speed

The smooth starting and stopping comes from a combination of Diesel-electric power, tight-lock couplers which eliminate slack between cars, roller bearings and electro-pneumatic disc brakes. Hydraulic shock-absorbers, resilient rubber cushioning and other unseen innovations combine to provide superb riding qualities.

Powerful Diesel engines are housed in the locomotive of the California Zephyr.

(Below) In the service they had been purchased for, passenger F-3 #9960C leads the westbound CALIFORNIA ZEPHYR across the IC diamond and out of Mendota. It is 1953 and within a year EMD E-units would be the regular power for the CZ. *(Mike Gleason)*

On February 1, 1953, the CB&Q began Vista-Dome ZEPHYR service between Chicago and Kansas City with the introduction of the KANSAS CITY ZEPHYR. This new ZEPHYR featured some new stainless steel equipment from the Budd Company, including a Vista-Dome parlor observation car and a Vista-Dome buffet coach, along with older pre-war Budd-built coaches and a baggage-mail car. Running as Trains #35 and 36, the KANSAS CITY ZEPHYR offered fast daytime schedules that were designed to compete with Santa Fe's passenger trains between the same cities.

(Top) The engineer on Train #35 has received the highball and has the KANSAS CITY ZEPHYR accelerating out of Mendota. Two E-8As are in charge today, while directly behind is a heavyweight baggage-RPO that has received a simulated stainless steel paint job and roller bearing truck journals for ZEPHYR service. The remaining four cars are Budd cars built for KCZ service.
(Mike Gleason)

(Bottom) It is 1954 and the KANSAS CITY ZEPHYR is in its second year of service. Train #35 has, only minutes before, left the Mendota depot and crossed over the tracks of the Illinois Central and Milwaukee Road as it proceeds west to Galesburg. The consist today is a complete and original KCZ, including Vista-Dome parlor-observation *Silver Terrace*.
(Mike Gleason)

(Top) Eastbound Train #6, the COLORADOAN, was due out of Mendota at 6:00 p.m. and scheduled to arrive at Chicago Union Station at 7:40 p.m. This schedule made COLORADOAN a popular train with people who had to be in Chicago the next morning for business. At times it would pick up an express car in Mendota. In this 1954 photo, an NW-2 has coupled onto the rear of #6 and is about to pull the train back to pick up the express car. The third car from the rear is one of the seven modernized heavyweight chair cars, numbered #4520-4526, which is painted in the simulated stainless steel scheme applied to at least 60 of the Burlington's heavyweight cars in the early 1950s. One of these modernized heavyweight chair cars could normally be found in the consist of the COLORADOAN.
(Mike Gleason)

Budd

(Bottom) Built by Budd in 1939 for the GENERAL PERSHING ZEPHYR, *Silver Star* was configured as a diner-parlor-observation and bore the facsimile of the famous General's signature on the drumhead. It was one of four such cars on the roster and could accomodate 24 patrons in the dining section and 22 customers in the parlor lounge. During the 1950s these cars saw regular service on the COLORADOAN. *Silver Star* was on Train #6, the eastbound COLORADOAN, at Mendota in this 1954 picture.
(Mike Gleason)

Zearing

(Right) E-8A #9944B leads the westbound CALIFORNIA ZEPHYR through Zearing in this July 1955 photo. The overpass, located at milepost 95.2, is the Burlington's branch that originally ran from Denrock to Streator. The line northwest of Zearing to Walnut was retired effective April 24, 1954.
(Mike Gleason)

(Below) On November 11, 1956, M-4A #6310, the class engine, leads a westbound freight past the small Q yard on the south side of the main at Zearing. The tracks on the far right are part of the New York Central's small yard at Zearing, the western-most track of the Central's Western Division and where the CB&Q and NYC interchanged traffic.
(R. W. Buhrmaster)

(Left) Master photographer Ray Buhrmaster caught up with #6310 as it coasted through Princeton, which is located eight miles west of Zearing. The fall grain rush of 1956 has this 2-10-4 working east of Galesburg. This would be the last year that steam would be used at harvest time. *(R.W. Buhrmaster)*

(Below) The mainline dispatcher has given #6310 the high green and the engineer has #6310 storming west out of Princeton and under the signal bridge at milepost 104.4. It will only take the mighty Colorado a few hours to cover the remaining 58 miles to Galesburg.   *(R. W. Buhrmaster)*

Princeton

The highway overpass at milepost 116.9 provided Ray Buhrmaster with an opportunity to catch #6310 banking through the curve and into the siding just west of the depot at Buda. Always a favorite photo location, the engine crews were accustomed to seeing photographers on the overpass. There was a small roundhouse and turntable in Buda to service the little steam engines that worked the branch that ran from Buda to Elmwood. The branch is behind the Chicago Bridge and Iron Works water tank on the right. *(R. W. Buhrmaster)*

As early as the 1850s, management of the CB&Q recognized that Galesburg would be the center of activity for the young railroad. By the late 1860s, the lines to Burlington, Quincy and Peoria were open and after the turn-of-the-century the lines south to the southern Illinois coal fields and north to the CB&N were contributing more traffic and revenues. Galesburg had become the hub of "Lines East."

With lines extending from Galesburg to Chicago, Peoria, Kansas City, St. Joseph, St. Paul, Omaha, Lincoln, Denver and into the southern Illinois coal fields, the railroad had to continually upgrade the facilities to keep up with demand. The yards, originally put into operation in 1906, were repeatedly enlarged and expanded along with a magnificent depot opened in 1912. A new 16-stall roundhouse was constructed in 1920, followed in 1924 by a car shop which was opened to build and repair freight cars, as was an adjacent wheel shop. In 1926 the new freight house was opened, replacing a like facility that dated back to 1865. Also during the 1920s, a 900-million gallon water reservoir was completed to quench the thirst of the hungry steam engines. The most ambitious program began in 1930 with the initiation of a three year project to completely rebuild the classification yards. Additionally, a new reefer icing facility was built, along with the construction of a massive concrete coaling tower, which would dominate the scene around the engine facilities. The roundhouse was expanded and became one of the largest on the entire system. As the demands of World War II traffic grew, the Burlington announced in June 1942 that it would double the size of the Galesburg yard, including hump facilities with retarders. Construction progressed at a furious pace and the new yard was operational by November 1942. The expanded yard had 114 miles of track, freight car capacity of 7,634, and was the largest facility of its kind on the entire railroad. And, in 1945, a new 135-foot turntable was installed at the roundhouse, simplifying the task of turning the largest steam locomotives on the road, the M-4A Colorados. The investment in fixed plant alone underlines the importance of Galesburg to the CB&Q. With the parade of passing ZEPHYRS and the constant activity at the roundhouse and in the yards, it was truly the heart of "Lines East."

(Above) Under the blistering sun of an August day in 1967, RPO #1942 awaits its next load of U.S. Mail. A 1922 product of Standard Steel Car Company, #1942 will be added to the consist of Train #47 which will depart Galesburg at 6:10 p.m. for a leisurely overnight trip to Rock Island, Savanna and the Twin Cities. *(Harold Ziehr)*

(Both) #5634, the next to last Class O-5A locomotive built at the railroad shops at West Burlington, leads a stock extra eastbound through the Galesburg depot in August 1954. With its consist from the Great Northern, Northern Pacific and the Burlington, the cars in this stock extra most likely originated from locations in Wyoming and Montana. The Burlington, serving all of the principal livestock markets, enjoyed an envied reputation for dependable livestock service. *(Joe Collias)*

(Above) On July 1, 1956, Class S-4A 4-6-4 #4000 was caught moving out from underneath the Galesburg concrete coal tower. Constructed by Baldwin in 1930 as #3002 and bearing builder number #61500, it would be rebuilt in 1937 and given a streamline shroud so that it could serve as standby power for the ZEPHYR fleet. Renumbered #4000, it would also be named *Aeolus*, after the Greek god, which means "Keeper of the Wind." It would only keep the stainless steel shroud until the first few months of 1942. Eleven years later it was outfitted with cab signals and Mars light in June 1953. *(R. W. Buhrmaster)*

(Left Only thirteen years old when this shot was taken in November 1953, O-5A #5631 is getting a load of black gold at the coaling tower. #5631 was assigned to the La Crosse Division and was regularly seen in La Crosse-Savanna-Galesburg and La Crosse-Savanna-Chicago service until 1956. *(Joe Collias)*

In the opinion of many railfans, the Fourth Street Bridge was the best location in Galesburg to take photos and capture the Q at work. These two shots, taken in November 1956 provide a panoramic view of Galesburg's engine facilities during the late 1950s.

(Above) On November 11, 1956, four unit FT #113A leads a manifest under the Fourth Street bridge and into the yard. Beyond the coaling tower is another F-unit lashup along with O-5A #5630. Class O-1A #4961 is under the tower while M-4A #6310 has just come out from beneath it. On the far right is another M-4A, #6326 while tank cars in diesel fuel service can be seen on the unloading siding on the far left. The scale track is between the fuel oil track and the FT-led freight. (R. W. Buhrmaster)

(Right) A few minutes later and with a full load of coal, O-1A #4961 is backing underneath the Fourth Street Bridge and toward the yard. A 1923 Baldwin product, #4961 sports one of the tenders with the coal bunker-sloped sides to improve visibility for switching duties.
(R.W. Buhrmaster)

The last shovelnose ZEPHYR unit constructed, built in April 1939, was #9908 and, unlike the earlier ZEPHYR power units, #9908 was the first and only one to have the EMC Blomberg six-wheel truck. Purchasing #9908 and a three car trainset to initiate ZEPHYR service between St. Louis and Kansas City, the Burlington elected to christen the train the GENERAL PERSHING ZEPHYR, since the train's route would be near the birthplace of the famous World War I General. The power unit, #9908, would be named *Silver Charger*, after the General's horse, *Charger*.

Silver Charger would see two ZEPHYR assignments during the early part of its career, the GENERAL PERSHING ZEPHYR and the OZARK STATE ZEPHYR. Beginning in the late 1940s, *Silver Charger* would work St. Louis-Burlington, Lincoln-St. Joseph, St. Louis-Burlington and finally Galesburg-Burlington. When photographed inside the Galesburg roundhouse in October 1963, *Silver Charger* was assigned to ferrying government guard cars between the passenger station at Burlington and the government arsenal at Dayman, Iowa. *(Bob Bullermann)*

(Top) A view of the turntable and roundhouse area at Galesburg in June 1964 reveals Class O-1A #4978 was outside, *Silver Charger* is occupying the stall on the left and Class O-1A #4960 is on the third roundhouse track. Also barely visible is a GP-7 and another steam engine to the right. *(Harold Ziehr)*

(Bottom) The Galesburg wheel plant was opened in 1924 as a temporary facility adjacent to the then-new Galesburg steel car shops. When the car shops closed in 1942, the wheel shop was to remain open until 1975, putting in 51 years of service. Using a wood combine body for the office \ locker room and a corrugated steel building for the machinery, the wheel plant would rework freight car wheelsets for CB&Q rip-tracks system-wide. Derrick #205225 was the *ex-officio* shop engine on site for decades. In this November, 1961 photo, it was dressed up in a green-black-silver livery by the shop foreman, Henry Page. *(Henry Page, David Van Drunen collection)*

Galesburg's M-4A 2-10-4's

When delivered by Baldwin between 1927 and 1929, the eighteen Class M-4 2-10-4 locomotives were designed to replace older 2-10-2s then working the southern Illinois coal drags. Assigned to the Galesburg and Beardstown Divisions, the new "Colorado" type engines increased tonnage per train and were capable of moving the drag freights more quickly over the line than the slower 2-10-2s.

In the middle 1930s, Burlington management elected to modernize the M-4 engines. With the intent being to convert the M-4 into a higher speed manifest freight locomotive, the shops at West Burlington installed Timken roller bearings, new Commonwealth one-piece steel cylinders, lightweight rods and new main drivers. All of the M-4 engines received these modifications from 1934 to 1940. Many of the M-4A engines were placed in manifest freight service between Lincoln, Nebraska and Denver, Colorado on "Lines West," which resulted in the class being dubbed the "Colorado" type.

The M-4 and M-4A engines also saw extensive "Lines East" service. As the F-units bumped the M-4A locomotives from mainline service on "Lines West," these displaced steam engines returned to the Galesburg and Beardstown Divisions and were common sights on the mainlines running between Galesburg-Pacific Junction and Galesburg-Centralia, and occasionally between Chicago-Galesburg. Most would continue in active service into 1958 and two would last until January 1959.

(Below) M-4A #6325 rides Galesburg's 135-foot turntable in this December 1955 photo clearly showing it has been outfitted with its distinctive Mars warning light. The next assignment for #6325 will most likely take it south to Beardstown and Centralia. *(Joe Collias)*

(Top) M-4A #6314, southbound with tonnage, is south of Galesburg on July 19, 1953. This November 1927 product of Baldwin Locomotive Works was upgraded to an M-4A in November 1939. *(Don Ball collection)*

(Center) M-4A #6316 moves through the Galesburg yard in this photo taken in August 1954. M-4A locomotives #6310-6315 were equipped with Elesco feedwater heaters, while #6316-6327 had Worthington-type BL heaters. #6316 has already received a Mars oscilliating warning light. *(Joe Collias)*

(Bottom) On the same day in August 1954, M-4A #6321 simmers at the Galesburg roundhouse. The last of the first order of twelve 2-10-4s acquired by the Burlington in 1927, #6321 sports a Worthington feedwater heater, but does not yet have a Mars light. *(Joe Collias)*

California Zephyr Exhibition Tour

In October 1945, management from the Burlington, Rio Grande and Western Pacific railroads authorized the purchase of 6 ten-car trains from the Edward G. Budd Manufacturing Company. The new stainless steel train, which would replace the heavyweight-equipped EXPOSITION FLYER, would feature Vista-Domes and would be called the CALIFORNIA ZEPHYR. By 1947 the consist had been lenghtened to eleven cars and the first cars would be delivered to the CB&Q in 1948. On March 24, 1948, the westbound EXPOSITION FLYER, Train #39, departed Chicago with one of the first CZ Vista-Dome coaches in the consist. As the sleepers and baggage cars were delivered, they too were placed in EXPOSITION FLYER service.

The new equipment continued to be delivered by Budd throughout 1948. In early 1949 it was apparent that full CALIFORNIA ZEPHYR service could commence that spring. Management of the three railroads agreed that exhibition trains, utilizing the CZ equipment, should go on display across their railroads prior to inauguaration of service. March 20th was chosen for commencement of CALIFORNIA ZEPHYR service, so the demonstration trains would conduct their on-line tours during the first two weeks of March 1949.

SOUVENIR
of a trip
CHICAGO to AURORA (Wye)
and Return
MARCH 19, 1949
aboard the
New California Zephyr
Featuring Vista-Domes

America's newest and most modern stainless steel, diesel-powered, streamlined train, embodying the latest travel comforts and conveniences, plus the most sensational of travel innovations ... Vista-Domes. In service daily between Chicago, Denver, Salt Lake City and San Francisco, via Burlington, Rio Grande and Western Pacific Railroads, commencing March 20, 1949.

NO EXTRA FARE ON ANY ZEPHYR

The World's Long Distance Non-Stop Record, 1017 Miles in 732 Minutes, 83.3 M.P.H., CHICAGO to DENVER, was made October 23, 1936 by a ZEPHYR.
* * *
America's First Diesel Streamlined Train Was The Pioneer Zephyr

(Below) The CALIFORNIA ZEPHYR exhibition train was on display in Galesburg during the first week of March 1949. While three-unit passenger F-3s had been purchased by the Burlington to power the CZ, E-5A #9915B was in charge for the exhibition tour which would make stops in Omaha, Lincoln, Burlington, Ottumwa, Des Moines and Chicago. *(Peter Van Drunen, David Van Drunen collection)*

(Above) The same day a set of Burlington F-units moves through the Galesburg depot and past the CALIFORNIA ZEPHYR exhibition train. The track going off to the right is the Quincy/Kansas City mainline.

(Below) CB&Q E-5A #9915B, the *Silver Clipper*, accelerates out of the Galesburg depot with the pre-inauguration CALIFORNIA ZEPHYR consist. CB&Q employee Peter Van Drunen photographed the train from the Seminary Street Tower. *(Both- Peter Van Drunen, David Van Drunen collection)*

Having completed its station stop in Galesburg, the KANSAS CITY ZEPHYR is accelerating out of the depot, past Seminary Street Tower and onto the Quincy main. Scheduled out of Galesburg at 3:03 p.m., it is due at West Quincy at 5:10 p.m. and Kansas City at 8:45 p.m. In this 1954 photo, the KCZ's consist includes Vista-Dome parlor-observation *Silver Terrace,* which could accomodate 27 parlor passengers and 24 patrons in the Vista-Dome. *(Mike Gleason)*

(Right) Motor car #9735 had been delivered as #735 to the Burlington by Pullman Car & Manufacturing Co. in 1929 and was upgraded with a 400 hp Lima-Hamilton diesel engine in 1949. In the late 1950s and into the early 1960s, #9735 could usually be found performing switching duties in Bushnell and Macomb, but in this photo was at the Galesburg roundhouse on April 5, 1959. *(M. Spoor collection)*

(Below) Built in July 1928 by Pullman Car & Manufacturing Co. as CB&Q #841 and renumbered two years later as #9841, it spent a considerable amount of time working on the Galesburg Division during the 1950s. During 1957-1959, #9841 was regularly assigned to Trains #147-148 running between Rock Island and Savanna. When these trains were discontinued on March 28, 1959, #9841 went back to Galesburg where it is photographed a week later on April 5, 1959. *(M. Spoor collection)*

Peoria

Chartered on the same day as the Aurora Branch, February 12, 1849, the Peoria and Oquawka Railroad aimed to build a rail line from Peoria west through Knox County and on to the Mississippi River. As events would unfold, the line would be built through Galesburg and arrive at the river, not at Oquawka, but across from the town of Burlington. Operations on the line began on March 17, 1855. Peoria has always been important for the CB&Q because traffic bound for the East was interchanged here with the New York Central and the Toledo, Peoria & Western.

(Top) For a number of years motor car #9772 and a trailer were the normal equipment for the Galesburg-Peoria trains. On June 11, 1956 it is approaching Peoria as Train #56. Built by Pullman in 1928 as #570, it was renumbered to #9570 and finally to #9772 in May 1930. It was rebuilt with a Lima-Hamilton 400 hp diesel in July 1949. *(M. Spoor collection)*.

(Center) On April 14, 1957, #9772 and trailer are at the small CB&Q depot in Peoria which was located at the foot of Edmund Street. It will depart for Galesburg at 8:00 p.m. and arrive an hour and a half later. *(R. W. Buhrmaster)*

(Bottom) Motor car #9772, running as Train #56, is about to arrive at the depot in Peoria in this photo taken on August 31, 1957. The Galesburg-Peoria trains would continue in operation until July 1, 1960. Motor car #9772 would remain on the roster until August 1966. *(M. Spoor collection)*

READ DOWN			56		Galesburg-Peoria			READ UP	
‡Bus Daily	‡Bus Daily	48 Daily	Ex. Sun. Motor	Mls.	Table No. 18	‡Bus Daily	‡Bus Daily	47 Daily	1 Ex. Sat. Motor
PM	PM	AM	AM			PM	PM	PM	PM
□ 7.35	□ 1.25	10.30	4.55	0	Lv. Galesburg, Ill. Ar	12.35	5.00	5 20	9 30
f	f	10.40	5.06	5	Knoxville			5 07	9 17
f	f	10.48		11	Gilson			4 58	f
8.00	1 55	10.55		16	Maquon	12.03	4.28	4 51	f 9.02
				20	Spoon River				
					Douglas			4 45	
8 12	2 09	/11.02	5.42	24	Ar. Yates City, 7	11 50	4 15	4 40	8 51
8.15	2.13	11.07	5.49	26	Lv. Elmwood, 19	11.47	4.12	PM	8 42
		AM	5.59	32	Oak Hill				8 32
f	f		f 6.11	39	Edwards	f	f		8 22
f	f			45	Pottstown	f	f		
+8.55	+2.50		6.40	53	Ar. Peoria, 7 🚋 Lv	+1110	+3 35		8.00
PM	PM		AM		Foot of Edmund St.	AM	PM		PM

Way of the Zephyrs

Wearing its as-delivered paint scheme with the large switcher herald, NW-2 #9215 was at work in Peoria on January 12, 1956. Crossing the tracks of the Toledo, Peoria & Western and the Peoria & Pekin Union, it is just a few blocks from the Peoria Union Station and the Burlington's roundhouse.
(M. Spoor collection)

GM
GENERAL MOTORS
DIESEL POWER

ELECTRO-MOTIVE DIVISION
GENERAL MOTORS
LA GRANGE, ILL.

Beardstown

As long as steam ruled the rails, an adequate supply of high grade coal was a necessity. In the early 1900s, the Burlington acquired a considerable number of acres in Franklin, Saline and Williamson Counties, as well as purchasing an existing 122 mile rail line running south of Concord to Centralia. Concord was a town on the existing Galesburg-East St. Louis line and only 18 miles south of Beardstown. Beardstown was picked for the division point, resulting in the facilities there being expanded to handle the expected growth in traffic.

(Below) On May 21, 1955, motor car #9844 is at Beardstown depot. Running as Train #12, the daily, except Sunday, motor car will depart at 6:45 a.m. for an all-stops, 188 mile run south on the Beardstown Division to Herrin. Upon arrival at 1:09 p.m., #9844 will have only a scant 6 minutes to be turned and readied for its 1:15 p.m. departure on the northbound run back to Beardstown. Constructed by Electro-Motive Corporation in July 1928 as CB&Q #844, this motor car would be renumbered to #9844 in 1930 and would continue in service until it was scrapped in August 1960. *(R.W.Buhrmaster)*

Chicago, Burlington & Quincy Railroad Company
LINES EAST OF THE MISSOURI RIVER

TIME TABLE

OF THE

BEARDSTOWN DIVISION

OF THE

EASTERN DISTRICT

No. 11

EFFECTIVE AT 12:01 A. M.
CENTRAL STANDARD TIME

SUNDAY, APRIL 9, 1950

DESTROY ALL TIME TABLES OF PREVIOUS DATE

This Time Table is for the exclusive use and guidance of the employes concerned, who must carry in addition thereto the Book of Rules of the Operating Department.

THE GUNTHORP-WARREN PRINTING COMPANY, CHICAGO

Distance from Concord	STATIONS
	..........CONCORD..........
	10.29
10.29	Wabash Crossing (Interlocked)
	0.20
10.49	......JACKSONVILLE.......
	0.10
10.59	.GM&O Crossing (Interlocked).
	6.81
17.40	..........PISGAH..........
	5.19
22.59	.........FRANKLIN.........
	5.87
28.46	.........WAVERLY.........
	6.42
34.88	..........LOWDER..........
	4.91
39.79	..........VIRDEN..........
	2.29
42.08	.I. T. Crossing (Auto. Interl.)...
	1.40
43.48	.GM&O Crossing (Interlocked).
	0.20
43.68	..........GIRARD..........
	8.40
52.08	.........ATWATER.........
	4.90
56.98	.........BARNETT.........
	6.29
63.27	.........LITCHFIELD.........
	0.20
63.47	..N. Y. C. Crossing (Interl.)...
	1.00
64.47	Wab. and I. C. Crossing (Interl.)
	6.71
71.18	.........WALSHVILLE.........
	5.80
76.98	N.Y.C. & St.L. Crossing (Interl.)
	..........SORENTO..........
	3.75
80.73	..........RENO..........
	3.34
84.07	..........AYERS..........
	7.92
91.99	P. R. R. Crossing (Interlocked)
	..........SMITHBORO..........
	5.11
97.10	.........HOOKDALE.........
	4.01
101.11	.........TAMALCO.........
	2.22
103.33	.........KEYESPORT.........
	4.24
107.57	..........BOULDER..........
	6.15
113.72	..........SHATTUC..........
	.B. & O. Crossing (Interlocked)
	6.10
119.82	......CENTRALIA YARD......
	......Southern Ry. Jct.......
	0.40
120.22	..........CENTRALIA..........
	.......SCHEDULED TIME.......
	.... AVERAGE MILES AN HOUR ...

Franklin

(Above) M-4A #6319 takes to the siding in Franklin as it rumbles past yet another of those steel water tanks. The date is July 1953 and #6319 is southbound with daily merchandise Train #70 bound for Centralia. *(Joe Collias)*

(Below) Leaning into the curve and pounding over the grade crossing at mile post 22.5, M-4A #6319 rattles the windows in the small, wood frame Franklin depot on this summer day in July 1953. Built in December 1927, it was rebuilt to M-4A specifications in February 1940 and would remain on the roster until May 1961. *(Joe Collias)*

Girard

Both the Gulf, Mobile & Ohio and the Illinois Terminal had grade level crossings with the Burlington in Girard. In this January 1952 photo, M-4A #6326 is at mile post 43.5 and is northbound with an extra freight consisting mostly of loaded hoppers bound for Galesburg.
(Don Ball collection)

Centralia

Centralia was the concentration point for coal coming out of the southern Illinois coal fields. With a 22 track yard consisting of 53 miles of track and a capacity for 2,400 cars, mine runs would be dispatched south to any of the 52 mines that the Burlington serviced in towns like West Frankfort, Herrin, Christopher and Ziegler. The mine runs, usually powered by one of the mighty M-4As or one of the older M-2As, would set out empties, pick up loads and return to Centralia.

(Below) In addition to the M-4A locomotives, there were a number of smaller Class O-1A Mikados used on the lines in the Illinois coal fields. In the mid 1950s, the O-1As would make their last stand working north out of Centralia to Shattuc and then west on the Baltimore & Ohio line from Shattuc to East St. Louis, where the Burlington trains cross the Mississippi and end up in the CB&Q yard in North St. Louis. On August 31, 1957, O-1As #4999 and #4980 were still at work in the yard at Centralia.
(R. W. Buhrmaster)

(Above) M-4A #6319 was awaiting its next assignment when photgraphed at the Centralia roundhouse in July 1953. The M-4As had a coal capacity of 24 tons and carried 21,500 gallons of water in their tenders. Many in the class, including #6319, had their tender water hatches moved forward to allow for standing room on either side. *(Joe Collias)*

(Below) #6327, the last of the eighteen 2-10-4s constructed, was at the Centralia roundhouse on August 24, 1957. With a maximum tractive effort of 90,000 pounds, these M-4As had no difficulty when routinely called upon to handle 8,800-ton coal trains. While most of the M-4As would see their fires doused in 1958, two would still be in service as late as January 1959.
(Max Zimmerlein collection)

(Above) In this photo taken in March 1958, O-1A #4997, M-4A #6317, and O-1A #5144 are gathered on the tracks adjacent to the Centralia roundhouse awaiting the call to duty that may never come.
(Joe Collias, Bob Bullermann collection)

(Below) On the same March day in 1958, O-1A #5090, its fires having been dropped and now vanquished to a lonely spot in the weeds, inspects the special duty SD-7s from EMD that have assumed command of the coal traffic on the Beardstown Division. The SD-7s arrived on the property from May through October 1953, and all were assigned to the coal country line south of Galesburg.
(Joe Collias, Bob Bullermann collection)

Class F-1 0-8-0 Switchers

The Burlington received ten Class F-1 0-8-0 switchers from the Brooks Works of the American Locomotive Company in 1919. Built in accordance with the United States Railroad Administration standards for 0-8-0 locomotives, the Class F-1 engines developed a tractive force of 50,600 lbs. These ten engines, numbered #540-549, would see extensive use in heavy switching assignments and were commonly found at work in the yards at Chicago, Cicero, Galesburg, Beardstown, Centralia and West Quincy.

(Top) In December 1951, F-1 #543 is waiting for a new switch list while working the yard in Centralia. Apparently, it has received a new Pyle headlight. Thirty-two years old when this photo was taken, #543 would be on the roster until 1956.
(Joe Collias)

(Bottom) Class F-1 #549, replete with a cuckoo clock headlight, is at work in Centralia in 1950. Centralia boasted of having four railroads: CB&Q, Illinois Central, Missouri-Illinois and Southern. The Burlington's yard was constantly busy handling strings of empty hoppers heading south and loaded hoppers bound for Galesburg, as well as interchanging traffic with the Southern.
(Bob Bullermann collection)

The level of train activity south of Centralia to the mines necessitated that the Burlington double track a considerable portion of the mainline. Much of this work was accomplished before 1917. From Centralia, the double track extended south to Zeigler Junction, a distance of 44 miles. Waltonville was midway between Centralia and Zeigler Junction and also the location where the Missouri Pacific crossed the CB&Q. Our last look at the M-4As is a going away shot of #6312 northbound at Waltonville on a cold, wintery November 9, 1957.
(Dick Wallin, Don Ball collection)

Hannibal Lines

Any coverage of "Lines East" would be incomplete without some tribute to the Burlington's line running south from Burlington along the west bank of the mighty Mississippi to St. Louis. This 221 mile stretch ran through Keokuk, Quincy and Hannibal, the town famous not for the railroad, but as the historic old-time river town and for the great American author, Samuel Clemens. The Burlington's tracks were laid along the same levee where Clemens began his career as a pilot of a Mississippi River steamboat.

Construction and acquistion of the line began at Burlington where the line to Keokuk was completed in 1856. There was no extension of this line southward, but in 1881 the CB&Q acquired the St. Louis, Keokuk and North Western, which ran from Mt. Pleasant, Iowa to Keokuk, hence south to Hannibal and Dardenne, where it joined the Wabash and enjoyed trackage rights into St. Louis. This acquisition allowed the CB&Q to enjoy a through route from St. Louis to Burlington where it connected with the CB&Q's major east-west mainline.

Under the sheltering bluffs; around the big bends . . . the way full of the tradition and the romance of a true American folklore which **Mark** Twain recorded for all the world to read.

In Hannibal is his boyhood home, and Becky Thatcher's home; the frame building where he learned the printer's craft; the cave where the buried treasure was found, and where Injun Joe died.

And always close alongside, the great river—the restless, mighty Mississippi . . . the wooded isles and the sand bars and the age-old levee.

As the train rounds a curve Yesterday and Today catch sight of each other. The flying Zephyr's sharp blast in salute to an old-timer is acknowledged by the deep-throated greeting of a Mississippi River side-wheeler.

(Right) Class R-5A #2062 heads a local freight through Wever, Iowa in August 1952. Originally constructed by Baldwin in 1906, it was rebuilt with new cylinders and Walschaerts valve gear in February 1927 and reclassified as an R-5A. This 2-6-2 would be retired three months after this photo was taken. *(Bernard Corbin, Corbin/Wagner collection)*

MARK TWAIN ZEPHYR

Burlington Route

NEW ROMANCE OF THE MISSISSIPPI VALLEY

(Below) On August 27, 1960, Train #44, with *Silver Charger* doing the honors, was running south along the mighty Mississippi River when photographed a little north of Keokuk. By this point, Train #44 was a nameless coach-only day train between Burlington and St. Louis. *(Barry Carlson)*

Keokuk

The MARK TWAIN ZEPHYR was the fourth articulated ZEPHYR trainset purchased by the Burlington, but the first ZEPHYR where the individual cars received names. Named after characters in Mark Twain's novels, the #9903, a 600 hp diesel/electric locomotive unit was named *Injun Joe*; the baggage car *Becky Thatcher*; the coach/dinette, *Huck Finn;* and the coach/observation car *Tom Sawyer*. The naming of the train, The MARK TWAIN ZEPHYR was appropriate, not only because of its St. Louis to Burlington, Iowa route along the Mississippi where Samuel Clemens piloted riverboats, but because Clemen's father was deeply involved in the formation of the Hannibal and St. Joseph Railroad, the oldest predecessor of the Burlington. Three days after its official christening by one of Clemen's granddaughters in Hannibal, Missouri on October 25, 1935, the MARK TWAIN ZEPHYR was placed in service. Here, almost 14 years later, it pauses briefly at the classic Keokuk, Iowa Union Depot in July of 1949. (*Charles Franzen*)

The MARK TWAIN ZEPHYR is not an excess fare train. Tickets at the lowest coach fares are honored in the 76 coach seats, while passengers riding in the parlor-lounge should hold transportation good for Pullman or parlor car travel.

NORTH Read Down No. 43	Miles	SCHEDULE of the MARK TWAIN ZEPHYR	SOUTH Read Up No. 44	One Way in Coaches	*One Way in Parlor Lounge	Round Trip in Coaches 10-day Limit	*Round Trip Parlor Lounge 10-day Limit	Seat in Parlor Lounge
AM 9.00	0	Lv. ....St. Louis...... Ar.	PM 9.10					
ƒ 9.04	2	......Washington Ave......	ƒ 8.59					
....ƒ....	15	......Spanish Lake......	....ƒ....	$ .30	$ .45	$ .54	$ .60	$ .50
....ƒ....	18	......Ft. Bellefontaine......	....ƒ....	.37	.55	.67	.75	.50
ƒ 9.29	20	......West Alton......	ƒ 8.33	.42	.62	.76	.85	.50
....ƒ....	27	......Machens......	....ƒ....	.55	.81	.99	1.10	.50
....ƒ....	34	......Orchard Farm......	....ƒ....	.68	1.01	1.23	1.35	.50
....ƒ....	43	......Peruque......	....ƒ....	.87	1.29	1.57	1.75	.50
10.07	52	......Old Monroe......	7.57	1.04	1.55	1.88	2.10	.50
10.13	56	......Winfield......	7.50	1.13	1.69	2.04	2.30	.50
....ƒ....	60	......Foley......	....ƒ....	1.20	1.79	2.16	2.40	.50
	62	......Oasis......		1.25	1.87	2.25	2.50	.50
	64	......Apex......		1.29	1.93	2.33	2.60	.50
.. 10.31	68	......Elsberry......	7.34	1.37	2.05	2.47	2.75	.50
....ƒ....	72	......Dameron......	....ƒ....	1.45	2.16	2.61	2.90	.50
....ƒ....	75	......Annada......	....ƒ....	1.52	2.27	2.74	3.05	.50
....ƒ....	79	......Kissenger......	....ƒ....	1.59	2.37	2.87	3.20	.50
10.53	84	......Clarksville......	7.14	1.69	2.53	3.05	3.40	.50
11.06	94	......Louisiana......	7.03	1.89	2.83	3.41	3.80	.50
	102	......Riverland......	ƒ	2.05	3.06	3.69	4.10	.50
11.18	104	......Ashburn......	6.49	2.09	3.13	3.77	4.20	.50
....ƒ....	107	......Busch......	....ƒ....	2.15	3.21	3.87	4.30	.50
....ƒ....	111	......Clemens......	....ƒ....	2.22	3.32	4.00	4.45	.50
11.43	113	......Saverton......	6.25	2.28	3.41	4.11	4.55	.50
11.53	120	Ar.).......Hannibal....... [Lv.	6.25	2.40	3.60	4.32	4.80	.50
	120	Lv.) [Ar.	6.15					
....ƒ....	134	......Mark......	....ƒ....					
12.18	140	Ar.).......Quincy, Ill. [Lv.	5.47	2.69	4.02	4.85	5.40	.60
12.24	140	Lv.) [Ar.	5.37	2.89	4.33	5.21	5.80	.60
12.38	150	......LaGrange......	5.20	3.00	4.50	5.40	6.00	.70
12.46	156	......Canton......	5.12	3.13	4.69	5.64	6.30	.70
	167	......Gregory......		3.34	5.00	6.02	6.70	.80
..n..	173	......Alexandria, Mo......	ƒ 4.49	3.46	5.18	6.23	6.95	.80
1.12	178	Ar.).......Keokuk, Ia. [Lv.	4.41	3.57	5.34	6.43	7.15	.80
1.18	178	Lv.) [Ar.	4.35					
1.32	189	......Montrose......	4.21	3.79	5.68	6.83	7.60	.95
1.47	202	......Ft. Madison......	4.06	4.05	6.06	7.29	8.10	.95
	210	......Wever......		4.20	6.30	7.56	8.40	.95
2.25	221	Ar. ......Burlington......Lv.	3.40	4.43	6.63	7.98	8.85	.95

* See last column for parlor seat fares. ƒ—Flag stop. n—Stops to leave revenue passengers.

Especial attention is invited to the fact that the MARK TWAIN ZEPHYR makes excellent connections at Burlington with the ARISTOCRAT for and from Omaha, Lincoln, Denver and California as well as for and from Chicago.

Westbound Read Down	THE ARISTOCRAT	Eastbound Read Up
10:30 AM	Lv............Chicago............Ar.	7:15 PM
3:00 PM	Ar...........Burlington...........Lv.	2:35 PM
3:04 PM	Lv...........Burlington...........Ar.	2:29 PM
11:00 PM	Ar............Omaha............Lv.	7:15 AM
12:55 AM	Ar............Lincoln............Lv.	5:35 AM
1:15 PM	Ar............Denver............Lv.	5:00 PM

Quincy and West Quincy

The CB&Q track between Galesburg and Quincy was opened on January 31, 1856, connecting the cities of Chicago and Quincy by rail for the first time. On the west bank of the Mississippi, track belonging to the Quincy and Palmyra Railroad was completed in 1860 to the connection with the Hannibal and St. Joseph, whose line to St. Joe had been completed in February 1859. On November 9, 1868, the first railroad bridge across the Mississippi at Quincy was opened, allowing direct rail service between Chicago and St. Joseph. The Burlington acquired the Hannibal & St. Joe on May 1, 1883, which had earlier purchased the Quincy and Palmyra. The result of these acquisitions was that the CB&Q had rail yards and depots in both Quincy, Illinois and across the river in West Quincy, Missouri.

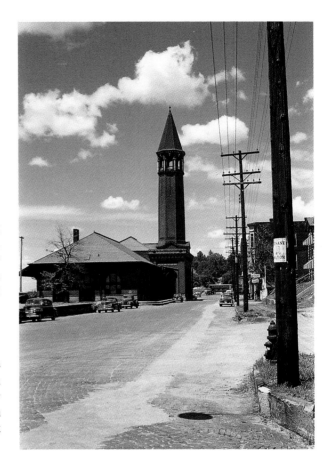

(Top) The Burlington had a majestic brick depot in Quincy, complete with a bell tower. The inefficiencies of having duplicate facilities on each side of the river sealed the fate of the Quincy depot, for when a new modern depot was opened in West Quincy in 1953, this wonderful station in Quincy was closed and demolished. Here it is seen in 1952 in its last year of operation. *(Bernand Corbin, Corbin/Wagner collection)*

(Bottom) FT-A #115A leads four other F-units past mile post 137 as they accelerate out of the West Quincy yard and past the depot. This is Train #74, an eastbound manifest freight, bound for Galesburg and Cicero. *(George Speir)*

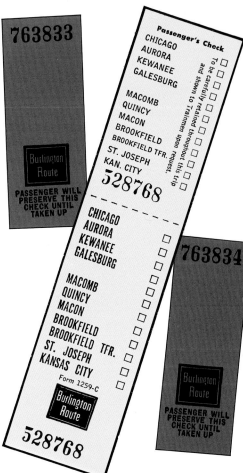

(Top) GP-7 #20 backs the *Silver Charger* towards its waiting train at the West Quincy depot in this April 1963 photo. Trains #1 and #44 had been reduced to running only between West Quincy and St. Louis as of November 1, 1960 and would be discontinued on April 28, 1963. *(George Speir)*

(Bottom) With its standard consist of a heavyweight baggage-RPO and a #6100 series heavyweight coach, *Silver Charger* accelerates out of the West Quincy depot on its southbound run to St. Louis as Train #44. It was scheduled to make a round trip to St. Louis and back, with departure at West Quincy scheduled for 5:40 p.m. and arrival in St. Louis at 9:20 p.m. An 11:20 p.m. departure from St. Louis would put #9908 back at the depot in West Quincy at 2:05 a.m. It would only operate for a few more weeks when this photo was taken in April 1963. *(George Speir)*

Hannibal

(Above) Positioned on the bluff just south of the downtown area, photographer Harold Ziehr has captured the Burlington's yard, roundhouse and shop facilities on film, as well as the offices of the Hannibal Division. Most of these structures were built by the Hannibal and St. Joseph Railroad before the turn of the century. *(Harold Ziehr)*

(Right) On May 6, 1961, F-7A #163A and GP-7's #244 and 255 were spotted next to the Hannibal water tank while awaiting their next assignment, which would be to power Train # 72 to North St. Louis later in the day. The employee timetable in effect when this photo was taken called for three daily southbound freights, with two terminating at West Alton and one continuing on to North St. Louis. *(M. Spoor collection)*

Old Monroe and Francis Subdivision

When the Burlington put the GENERAL PERSHING ZEPHYR into service between St. Louis and Kansas City in 1938, its route took it north out of St. Louis over the CB&Q to Old Monroe. There it left the St. Louis-Hannibal main and turned west over the Old Monroe and Francis Subdivision to Wellsville, where a joint trackage agreement with the Wabash began for the remaining 17 miles to Francis. Two miles of running on Gulf, Mobile & Ohio trackage brought the train to the depot in Mexico, Missouri. From Mexico to Kansas City the CB&Q operated over trackage rights obtained from the GM&O.

(Above) The Burlington operated a mixed train between Old Monroe and Mexico which connected at Old Monroe with the MARK TWAIN ZEPHYR. Operating westbound from Old Monroe as Train #123, it is seen here in July 1957 at the depot in Mexico. Scheduled for a 1:30 p.m. arrival in Mexico, it would complete its work, turn and depart at 2:05 p.m as Train #124 for the 65 mile trip to Old Monroe.   *(Homer Benton, M. Spoor collection)*

Old Monroe and Francis
TIME TABLE No. 93.

Distance from St. Louis	Distance from Old Monroe	STATIONS	Distance from Francis	Sidings	Other Tracks
51.6		.......OLD MONROE.......	63.0	Storage 26	29
		——4.6——			
56.2	4.6	.........ETHLYN.........	58 4		15
		——5.1——			
61.3	9.7	........MOSCOW........	53.3	50	11
		——4.2——			
65 5	13 9	.......SOUTH TROY.......	49 1		19
		——7.4——			
72.9	21.3	.......HAWK POINT.......	41.7		22
		——5.8——			
78 7	27.1	.....NEW TRUXTON......	35 9		7
		——6.5——			
85.2	33 6	...LIEGE-BELLFLOWER...	29.4		32
		——5.4——			
90 6	39 0	.........BUELL.........	24.0		12
		——7.6——			
98.2	46 6	.......WELLSVILLE.......	16.4	29	11
		——5.0——			
103 2	51.6	.......MARTINSBURG......	11.4	27	
		——6.4——			
109 6	58.0	.........HAIG.........	5.0	26	
		——5.0——			
114.6	63.0	........FRANCIS........		No. 1 13	Yard

Hannibal to St. Louis
TIME TABLE No. 93.

Distance from Hannibal	STATIONS
119.7	........UNION STATION........
	————3.9————
115.8	.....NORTH MARKET........
	Wabash Crossing (Interlocked)
	Wiggins Crossing (Interlocked)
	————3.3————
112.5	.....NORTH ST. LOUIS.......
	————2.2————
110.3	..........BADEN............
	————1.0————
109.3	......PROSPECT HILL.......
	————4.5————
104.8	.....SPANISH LAKE........
	————5.5————
99.3	........WEST ALTON........
	————6.5————
92.8	.........MACHENS..........
	(Interlocked)
	————2.1————
90.7	.........PERKINS..........

Chicago, Burlington & Quincy Railroad Company

LINES EAST OF THE MISSOURI RIVER

TIME TABLE

93

OF THE

HANNIBAL DIVISION

OF THE

CENTRAL DISTRICT

No. 93

EFFECTIVE AT 12:01 A. M.
CENTRAL STANDARD TIME

SUNDAY, FEBRUARY 1, 1953

DESTROY ALL TIME TABLES OF PREVIOUS DATE

This Timetable is for the exclusive use and guidance of the employes concerned, who must carry in addition thereto the Book of Rules of the Operating Department.

STANDARD PRINTING CO., HANNIBAL, MO.

St. Louis

While not one of the first cities you would think of when reflecting on Burlington's ZEPHYR passenger trains, St. Louis could claim four of the stainless steel streamliners: GENERAL PERSHING ZEPHYR, OZARK STATE ZEPHYR, MARK TWAIN ZEPHYR and ZEPHYR ROCKET. Additionally, there were secondary passenger trains to Burlington and Galesburg. In December 1957, E-7A #9949, another E-7A and an E-8A lead a troop train through the double slip switches as it nears the huge train shed of St. Louis Union Station. *(Richard A. Wolter)*

Across Missouri

(Above) Macon, Missouri, an agriculturally focused community 68 miles west of West Quincy, was a stop for all of the passenger trains running across the Hannibal & St. Joseph Railroad. On July 9, 1957, the MARK TWAIN ZEPHYR, running as Train #3, is stopped at the town's depot. Train #3 was the all-stops local between West Quincy and St. Joseph whose primary purpose was to provide connecting service for passengers leaving the KANSAS CITY ZEPHYR at Brookfield but were continuing on to St. Joseph. *(Don Ball collection)*

**West Quincy,
Hannibal
and Brookfield**
TIME TABLE No. 93.

Mile Post Location	STATIONS
2.2	WEST QUINCY
	3.9
6.1	MARK
	2.9
9.0	NORTH RIVER
	5.5
14.5	PALMYRA
	HANNIBAL
	0.3
0.3	Wabash Crossing (Grade)
	HANNIBAL U. D.
	5.9
6.2	WHITE BEAR
	1.8
8.0	WITHER'S MILL
	6.8
14.8	PALMYRA
	4.2
19.0	WOODLAND
	4.7
23 7	ELY
	6.4
30.1	MONROE CITY

(Left) Five miles west of Macon was the small town of Bevier where the Burlington interchanged with the small coal hauling Bevier & Southern Railway. For a number of years the B&S Ry was a major source of revenue for the Q. GP-7 #246, with an eastbound freight on February 6, 1959, is seen here passing the B&S Railway water tank which had previously belonged to the CB&Q. The composite gondolas on the siding had been set out earlier by the shortline. *(F. Hol Wagner, Jr.)*

Brookfield

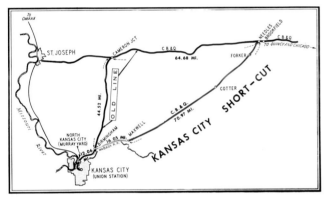

Brookfield, 100 miles from West Quincy and 105 miles from St. Joseph, was originally reached by the Hannibal & St. Joe in 1858 and became the division point and the site of a roundhouse, shop facility and classification yard. In 1949 Brookfield gained a more prominent role when management announced that the Burlington would relocate and rebuild its Kansas City line. The original line via Cameron Junction, Missouri had been completed in 1869 and provided the first through trains between Chicago and Kansas City. However the line was 478 miles long whereas the competing lines were as short as 450 miles. The answer was to relocate the line and shorten the Chicago-Kansas City route by 22.2 miles. The new Kansas City Short-Cut would leave the West Quincy / St. Joe main just west of Brookfield at Needles and proceed down the rebuilt Carrolton Branch and on to newly built track between Cotter and Maxwell, a distance of 42.6 miles. The Kansas City Short-Cut opened for freight traffic in October 1952 and passenger traffic in 1953, with the introduction on February 1, 1953 of two new Vista-Dome streamliners, the daytime KANSAS CITY ZEPHYR and the overnight AMERICAN ROYAL ZEPHYR.

(Above) In this photo taken on October 4, 1958, we find gas-electric #9767 resting next to the stone enginehouse built by the Hannibal & St. Joe. The gas-electric operated as Trains #35-3 westbound and #4-36 eastbound and provided the connection between Brookfield and St. Joseph for the KANSAS CITY ZEPHYR. When the passengers from the KCZ crossed the platform and were all aboard, the gas-electric departed for St. Joseph at 6:55 p.m. Today the gas-electric is pulling coach #6000, the one-of-a-kind *Silver Pendulum* built by Pacific Railway Equipment Company in January 1942.
(Bernard Corbin, Corbin/Wagner collection)

(Right) When the gas-electric was undergoing monthly maintenance, a GP-7 would fill in on the run between St. Joseph and Brookfield. Such was the case on this day in June 1958. Just west of Brookfield, GP-7 #260 hustles Train #35-3 towards its 9:59 p.m. arrival in St. Joseph. With the gas-electric out of service, the train has picked up a heavyweight baggage-mail car in addition to the normally assigned *Silver Pendulum*. *(M. Spoor collection)*

St. Joseph

Mid morning was the busiest time of the day at the St. Joseph Union Depot in terms of arriving and departing Burlington passenger trains. The peak activity was between 10:00 a.m. and 11:00 a.m. Trains would be arriving from Chicago, Kansas City and Creston, while departing trains would be bound for Chicago, Kansas City, Omaha and Lincoln.

(Below) On a bitter cold morning in December 1957, Dick Wolter was on hand to record the parade of Burlington passenger trains. On the far left, a Phase 1 E-7A is the power on northbound Train #27 which arrived from Kansas City at 10:40 a.m. and is due to depart for Omaha and Lincoln at 10:50 a.m. Next to #27 is the PIONEER ZEPHYR, which has spent the night in St. Joseph and is now being readied for its 11:05 a.m. departure for Lincoln via Table Rock and Wymore as Train #41. E-8A #9973 brought the overnight AMERICAN ROYAL ZEPHYR in from Chicago at 8:20 a.m. On the track closest to the depot is a gas-electric that has come in from Creston, Iowa as Train #30 at 10:30 a.m. Passengers arriving on Train #30 who are bound for Kansas City will have to wait until 11:35 a.m. when their connection, Train #20, the SILVER STREAK ZEPHYR, arrives from Lincoln and Omaha. The SILVER STREAK ZEPHYR will depart for Kansas City at 11:43 a.m. *(Richard A. Wolter)*

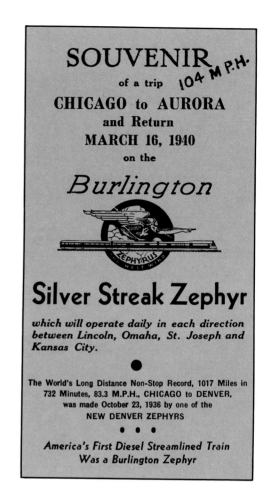

SOUVENIR *104 M.P.H.*
of a trip
CHICAGO to AURORA
and Return
MARCH 16, 1940
on the

Burlington

Silver Streak Zephyr

which will operate daily in each direction between Lincoln, Omaha, St. Joseph and Kansas City.

●

The World's Long Distance Non-Stop Record, 1017 Miles in 732 Minutes, 83.3 M.P.H., CHICAGO to DENVER, was made October 23, 1936 by one of the NEW DENVER ZEPHYRS

● ● ●

America's First Diesel Streamlined Train Was a Burlington Zephyr

The PIONEER Zephyr

America's First Diesel-Powered Streamlined Train...

By the scheduled 11:05 a.m. departure of the PIONEER ZEPHYR, Train #4-36 has already departed at 10:50 a.m. for Brookfield and its connection with the KANSAS CITY ZEPHYR and Train #27 has left at 10:55 a.m. for Omaha and Lincoln. Here the PIONEER ZEPHYR, left alone under the St. Joe Union Depot trainshed, waits for its 11:05 a.m. departure time. *(Both- Richard A. Wolter)*

(Left) On the morning of February 15, 1958, motorcar #9767, operating as Train #4-36, is leaving St. Joseph for Brookfield. This motor car was unique with its silver paint that matched the equally unique *Silver Pendulum*.
(Bernard Corbin, Corbin/Wagner collection)

(Below) The next day, EMD SW-7 #9265 readies the #9767 for yet another trip to Brookfield. The motor car had returned from Brookfield at 9:59 p.m. the night before.
(Bernard Corbin, Corbin/Wagner collection)

(Top) A year and a few weeks later, on March 7, 1959, #9767 and *Silver Pendulum* are again leaving St Joe as Train 4-36.
(Bernard Corbin, Corbin/Wagner collection)

(Center) Two days later SW-7 #9266, a July 1950 EMD product, switches #9908, the *Silver Charger*. For most of the period 1958-1960, *Silver Charger* was assigned to St. Joseph-Lincoln service. *(Bernard Corbin, Corbin/Wagner collection)*

(Below) On the morning of June 1, 1959, motor car #9767 is again at the Union Depot in St. Joseph, awaiting its 10:55 a.m. departure for Brookfield. In the background, the rear of the PIONEER ZEPHYR's observation car can be seen. The little ZEPHYR had arrived from Lincoln as Train #44 at 4:10 in the morning and is waiting for its 11:10 a.m. departure from St. Joe as Train #41. It will hold this assignment for a little more than nine more months and on March 20, 1960 will make its last run from Lincoln to Chicago and its permanent home at the Museum of Science and Industry. *(Charles Franzen)*

Burlington

What would the Burlington Route, the CB&Q, be without the city of Burlington, Iowa? Burlington, Iowa had been around for less than 20 years when, in 1852, the rails of the Peoria & Oquawka pushed eastward from the banks of the Mississippi to Galesburg, followed shortly thereafter by the Burlington and Missouri River Rail Road, building westward from Burlington to Omaha. The two Burlingtons "grew-up" together. The Mississippi River was bridged in 1868, and by the mid-1870s eleven different railroad companies would serve Burlington, with rails reaching out in all directions. But the CB&Q has always been the primary railroad in Burlington and an integral part of that city. CB&Q President Charles Perkins called Burlington his home and adopted its name for the familiar "Burlington Route" moniker for the railroad's advertising.

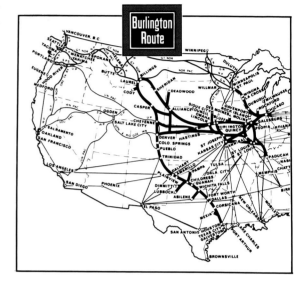

From the magnificent double track steel drawbridge over the Mississippi, around the two sharpest curves on the Chicago to Denver mainline between Chicago and Omaha, down the "K-line" hugging the 160-foot bluffs on the Iowa side of the river, past the landmark railroad-built grain elevator and the modern Lannon-stone Union Depot, up the famous West Burlington hill and beyond the West Burlington Shops, the drama of Burlington railroading has always enjoyed a well-equipped stage.

(Below) The use of gas-electric passenger motor cars -- "doodlebugs" -- on the Q began in the mid1920s. At least five motor car runs originated at Burlington, Iowa over the lightly traveled branch lines that fanned out in all directions. The Washington, Oskaloosa and Carrollton locals, the "Dolly" from Burlington to Galesburg via Aledo and the Quincy local via Carthage, all provided passenger service with the sputtering motor cars. Motor car #9816, a 275 hp coach/baggage/mail car, rests on one of the stub tracks at the south end of the Burlington, Iowa depot surrounded by RPOs being loaded along with a string of diesel fuel tank cars. At 3:45 in the afternoon, the little doodlebug would depart Burlington with two short, anemic blats from its single-note air horns and head down the east side of the river, through Carthage, to Quincy, as Train #110. *(Jim Ewinger)*

(Above) Burlington's MARK TWAIN ZEPHYR rests on track 1 of the Burlington, Iowa depot in the early 1950s. Just before arriving in Burlington, the four-car articulated train would be turned on a wye specifically built for it, and then backed the last mile into the station. Because the rails hug the bluffs of the river here, the wye had to be located in a narrow ravine. As Train #43, the ZEPHYR was scheduled to depart St. Louis at 8:30 in the morning, with a Burlington arrival at 2:20 p.m. The MTZ would be serviced, and then depart as Train #44, at 4:00 p.m., to arrive home in St. Louis at 9:58 p.m. The schedule of the MTZ was one of the slowest of the ZEPHYR fleet despite scheduled speeds of 80 mph. It averaged only 42 mph on its 442 mile round trip from St. Louis because of the sixty stops along the way. *(Jim Ewinger)*

(Right) A pair of stainless steel E5s, with #9915B in the lead, head the exhibition run of the CALIFORNIA ZEPHYR as it leaves the depot at Burlington, Iowa on its way back to Chicago. It is the second week of March 1949, and within a week, the CZ will commence regular service. *(Jim Ewinger)*

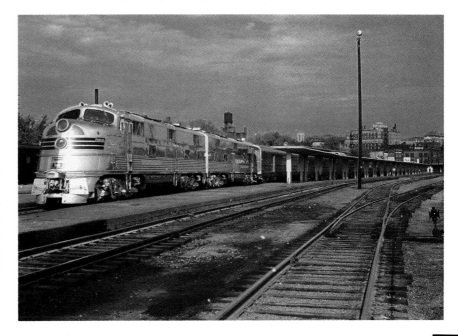

The topography of Burlington's "Lines East" varied from the almost level route across Illinois and up the Mississippi to the Twin Cities, to the rolling hills of northern Missouri and southern Iowa. Several "helper districts" were warranted in the latter areas, which provided quite a show for railfans during the steam era. This sequence of color photos starting in the Burlington, Iowa yards follows M-2A #6138 helping road engine O-5A #5617 lift its freight to the top of the West Burlington Hill. Even though these late autumn views from the early 1950s are magnificent, they are barely adequate to capture the drama of a pair of steam locomotives laboring up the hill. It was customary for steam locomotives having received class repairs at the Burlington Shops, to spend time in helper service during their "break-in" period. However, here, in the last days of steam on the Burlington, that is not the case. #6138 would soon be scrapped, during October of 1953, and the West Burlington-built Northern would follow seven years later. *(All- Jim Ewinger)*

(Above) In 1953 the two stainless steel baggage cars purchased for the NEBRASKA ZEPHYR, the *Argo* and *Olympus,* were reassigned to the DENVER ZEPHYR and replaced with a pair of 70-foot 990-series smooth-sided "economy" baggage cars. Burlington's own forces at Havelock, Nebraska had built these cars in 1951 and adorned them with the simulated stainless steel shadow-line aluminum paint scheme. One of these cars is in the consist today, as an E-7A pilots the NEBRASKA ZEPHYR through Burlington, Iowa. *(Jim Ewinger)*

THE
NEBRASKA
Zephyr

Completely Streamlined
Diesel-Powered · Stainless Steel

∗ ∗ ∗

Fast Daytime Service
between

CHICAGO - OMAHA - LINCOLN

∗ ∗ ∗

Convenient Mid-Day Departure
WESTBOUND AND EASTBOUND

Burlington
Route

THE
NEBRASKA
Zephyr

New *Zephyr* Service
between
CHICAGO-OMAHA-LINCOLN

(Left) Having just departed the depot, Train #18, the CALIFORNIA ZEPHYR, passes through the yards at Burlington, Iowa and approaches the sharp curve that leads to the Mississippi River bridge. The CZ today is led by E-8A #9941B. *(Jim Ewinger)*

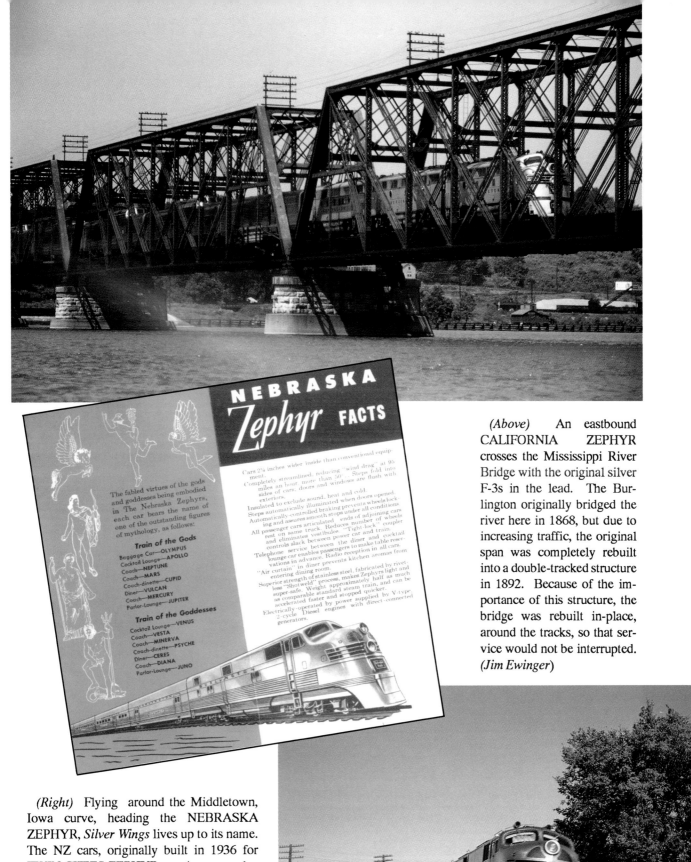

NEBRASKA Zephyr FACTS

The fabled virtues of the gods and goddesses being embodied in The Nebraska Zephyrs, each car bears the name of one of the outstanding figures of mythology, as follows:

Train of the Gods
Baggage Car—OLYMPUS
Cocktail Lounge—APOLLO
Coach—NEPTUNE
Coach—MARS
Coach-dinette—CUPID
Diner—VULCAN
Coach—MERCURY
Parlor-Lounge—JUPITER

Train of the Goddesses
Cocktail Lounge—VENUS
Coach—VESTA
Coach—MINERVA
Coach-dinette—PSYCHE
Diner—CERES
Coach—DIANA
Parlor-Lounge—JUNO

Cars 2¼ inches wider inside than conventional equipment.
Completely streamlined, reducing "wind drag" at 95 miles an hour, more than 50%. Steps fold into sides of cars, doors and windows are flush with exteriors.
Insulated to exclude sound, heat and cold.
Steps automatically illuminated when doors opened.
Automatically-controlled braking prevents wheels locking and assures smooth stops under all conditions.
All passenger cars articulated—ends of adjoining cars rest on same truck. Reduces number of wheels and eliminates vestibules. "Tight-lock" coupler controls slack between power car and train.
Telephone service between the diner and cocktail lounge car enables passengers to make table reservations in advance. Radio reception in all cars.
"Air curtain" in diner prevents kitchen aromas from entering dining room.
Superior strength of stainless steel, fabricated by rivetless "Shotweld" process, makes Zephyrs light and super-safe. Weight approximately half as much as comparable standard steam train, and can be accelerated faster and stopped quicker.
Electrically-operated by power supplied by V-type 2-cycle Diesel engines with direct-connected generators.

(Above) An eastbound CALIFORNIA ZEPHYR crosses the Mississippi River Bridge with the original silver F-3s in the lead. The Burlington originally bridged the river here in 1868, but due to increasing traffic, the original span was completely rebuilt into a double-tracked structure in 1892. Because of the importance of this structure, the bridge was rebuilt in-place, around the tracks, so that service would not be interrupted. *(Jim Ewinger)*

(Right) Flying around the Middletown, Iowa curve, heading the NEBRASKA ZEPHYR, *Silver Wings* lives up to its name. The NZ cars, originally built in 1936 for TWIN CITIES ZEPHYR service, were also named after Greek gods and goddesses and provided Chicago-Lincoln service from November 1947 through January 1968. #9913 was from the second batch of stainless steel E-5s the Burlington purchased from EMD. *(Jim Ewinger)*

The Burlington to Washington branch line was started as the Burlington and Northwestern Narrow Gauge Railway in 1876 and completed to Washington in 1880. For the first 14 miles out of Burlington, the line obtained trackage rights over what would become the Rock Island and used a third rail placed between two standard gauge rails for its 3-foot gauge equipment. On June 29, 1901, the entire B&NW, along with the Winfield to Oskaloosa branch, was widened to standard gauge. Approximately 125 miles of 3-foot gauge track was widened to the standard 4 foot, 8 1/2 inches in one day, virtually all between daybreak and dusk. These lines would be the last narrow gauge lines in Iowa to be converted to standard gauge; all others would just be abandoned.

Operations on the B&NW, even after the 1901 absorption into the CB&Q, remained bucolic until mixed service over the line was discontinued. It was not uncommon for the crews to stop anywhere along the line to accommodate regular passengers. Steam locomotives handled both freight and passenger trains until 1928, when passenger operations were taken over by the doodlebugs. After downgrading passenger service to mixed trains, the doodlebugs disappeared and most trains were run with "P" class Atlantic type engines. Occasionally a "K" class ten wheeler or an "H" class Mogul would be summoned from the Burlington roundhouse to handle the run. These engines were well up to the task of handling the small trains over the line. During the early 50s, one of the Burlington yard's diesel switch engines would frequently handle the short turn to Washington over the branches light rail. After the final steam powered train in August of 1953, Burlington SW-1 and NW-2 switchers would take over the run almost exclusively, with an infrequent train powered by a GP-7 or a GP-9.

(Above) The terminus of the Burlington rails in Washington was a wye with the Burlington depot between the legs and a small stock yard on the north leg that interchanged with the Rock Island branch line to Des Moines. Charles Franzen began photographing the Washington railroads after WWII and caught the last days of steam and the early days of diesel on the branch in color. Class P6A class Atlantic #2593 rests on the wye near the depot in July of 1949. This locomotive was built by Rogers in 1903 for the St. Louis, Keokuk and Northwestern, an early Burlington subsidiary, as number #784. In 1928 it was rebuilt with new 69" drivers replacing the 78" drivers which were used when it was in mainline passenger service, assigned her present number and downgraded to branchline service. In a short 18 months this locomotive would be scrapped. *(Charles Franzen)*

Burlington Route

(Right) Class P6 Atlantic #2584 has just delivered a long string of boxcars to Washington. This locomotive was built by Baldwin in 1905 as #2714, and was rebuilt with smaller diameter drivers in 1928. Occasionally, the train crew would park the train on the west leg of the wye and walk to a trackside cafe for lunch prior to their return to Burlington.
(Charles Franzen)

(Below) Atlantics were the primary source of power on the Washington branch mixed during the last days of steam. Here, the #2584 works in Washington in September of 1953, just 18 months before it would be scrapped. Before long, the familiar sights and sounds of steam huffing and puffing through Washington would be replaced by the chanting of diesel power in the form of black and gray switchers with red and yellow stripes. *(Charles Franzen)*

Albia, Iowa, at milepost 303.71 west of Chicago, was the only rail connection for Burlington passengers from Iowa's capital, Des Moines, after the late 1940s. The daily, except-Sunday, mixed's early 7:15 a.m. departure from Des Moines, placed passengers in Albia at 11:00 a.m. It turned and departed in only a half-hour, returning to Des Moines by 2:45 that same afternoon. Photographer Michael Joynt rode the Albia local in April 1957, and recorded these scenes of the Q in this south-central Iowa community.

(Above) Waiting impatiently to proceed southbound on the joint Burlington-Wabash tracks between Tracy and Albia, the northbound Wabash freight must clear before Train #28 may proceed. Headed by locomotive #267, the highest numbered GP7 on the Burlington roster, the mixed consists today of a composite gondola, an ancient, wooden Q stock car, a GN reefer and finally the combine. *(Michael P. Joynt)*

(Bottom) At 3:41 that afternoon, eastbound Train #12, the NEBRASKA ZEPHYR, stopped briefly at the Albia depot. Usually headed by only one of the Q's silver E7 locomotives, like #9928B, the seven-car, fully articulated, stainless steel trains of the gods and goddesses, flew across Iowa in only four and a half hours, making twelve stops along the way. Today, one of the stainless steel baggage cars, either *Argo* or *Olympus*, is tucked in behind the locomotive. *(Michael P. Joynt)*

(Above and right) An hour later, the westbound COLORADOAN stops at Albia. Several remnants of passing eras are evident in these two views. The lower quadrant semaphore in the background, the mail crane to the right of the train, the red REA sign on the end of the depot, the baggage carts on the classic Q herringbone brick platform, the heavyweight passenger equipment and even the COLORADOAN itself, would soon disappear from the railroading scene. The Burlington painted over sixty pieces of older heavyweight equipment with simulated stainless steel shadow lining in an attempt to better match the more modern ZEPHYR equipment. Bringing up the markers of a train loaded with front-end mail business, is heavyweight lounge/diner #307 or #308, preceded by a modernized 6100-series coach and a long string of baggage and mail cars. The protecting trainman on the platform is not quite the prescribed distance from the end of his train, but the brief stop here did not afford the opportunity to follow the rule to the letter. (Both- Michael P. Joynt)

Red Oak

Red Oak is 50 miles west of the division point at Creston and 32 miles east of Pacific Junction. It was a busy junction, with branch lines running 19 miles north to the agricultural town of Griswold and 39 miles southwest to Hamburg where the line met the Kansas City-Council Bluffs mainline.

(Opposite page, top and bottom) In these March 1951 views, photographer Bernard Corbin has captured the character of the Burlington. Baggage cars are loaded and awaiting the next Chicago-Council Bluffs passenger train. Burlington Class K-2 4-6-0 #654 awaits its next assignment. Constructed in February 1893 by Rogers, #654 is only a few months away from its retirement in June 1951. When stricken from the roster, it will have worked 58 years for the CB&Q and its predecessor in Iowa, the Burlington and Missouri River.
(Both - Bernard Corbin, Corbin/Wagner collection)

The NEBRASKA Zephyr
One of America's Distinctive Trains

The Nebraska Zephyr brings new comfort, convenience and luxury to Burlington's daytime travelers between Chicago, Omaha and Lincoln. Diesel-powered, streamlined and built of stainless steel, the Nebraska Zephyr combines the smooth speed, for which all Zephyrs are famous, with spaciousness, comfort and elegance.

The Nebraska Zephyr is composed of a richly-appointed parlor car providing a spacious private drawing-room (berth can be made down if desired) and a cozy observation-lounge . . . a beautiful dining car . . . three chair coaches and a dinette-coach . . . a smartly-styled cocktail lounge . . . and a powerful Diesel-electric locomotive.

Throughout this completely air-conditioned train, colorful decoration adds a cheerful note to sleek, modern design. Windows, with sills at elbow height, are double-width, mist-proof and frost-proof. Seats are scientifically designed for maximum comfort. Lighting is restfully diffused. Telephone service between the diner and cocktail lounge car enables passengers to make advance table reservations. Radio reception in all cars.

Each of the two trains required for this service makes one daily trip between Chicago, Omaha and Lincoln—a distance of 551 miles. Diesel-powered for smooth, effortless speed, they cruise at 80 to 90 miles per hour.

Articulation and tight-lock coupling eliminate slack between cars and afford velvet-smooth starting and stopping. Roller bearings, low center of gravity, electro-pneumatic brakes, a smooth roadbed—all are reflected in the superb riding comfort of this train.

Porter service is available to coach and parlor car passengers.

The Nebraska Zephyr Is Not An Extra-Fare Train!

(Below) On December 28, 1957, the NEBRASKA ZEPHYR, with E-5A #9915A on the point, rolls eastward near Red Oak. Somewhat unusual is the presence of a second diesel locomotive. During the 1950s, Trains #11 and #12 normally operated with only one unit.
(Bernard Corbin, Corbin/Wagner collection)

(Top) Three E-7s lead the eastbound Train #6-12, the combined NEBRASKA ZEPHYR and COLORADOAN at milepost 441, about a mile and a half east of Red Oak. The two trains had begun operating as a combined train between Chicago and Omaha on February 1, 1958, just four months before this photo was taken on May 24, 1958. Prior to the combining of the two trains, the NZ would rarely have had heavyweight head-end cars in its consist. *(Bernard Corbin, Corbin/Wagner collection)*

(Bottom) A four-unit F-3, with #126D in the lead, rolls tonnage east, just a mile east of Red Oak on August 3, 1958. *(Bernard Corbin, Corbin/Wagner collection)*

(Above) Mixed train service was provided to Griswold to the north and Hamburg to the south. GP-7 #202, with one of the branch line heavyweight combines, awaits its call. When this photo was taken on July 2, 1958, mixed Train #101 ran daily, except Sunday, to Hamburg. *(Bernard Corbin, Corbin/Wagner collection)*

(Right) For years the Burlington assigned General Electric 44-ton switchers to work the branches north and south out of Red Oak. On April 26, 1959, #9104 rests between assignments at Red Oak where it was assigned for a number of years.
(Bernard Corbin, Corbin/Wagner collection)

Pacific Junction

"Lines East" start in Chicago, but where do they end? Located 475.48 miles from the Windy City, Pacific Junction, Missouri is where "Lines East" meet "Lines West" and where the east-west mainline between Chicago and Denver crosses the north-south line running between Council Bluffs and Kansas City. Just 3.8 miles east of the Burlington's crossing of the Missouri River, "P. Junc." was the site of a modest freight yard, engine facilities and a Burlington Refrigerator Express icing facility.

(Below) Until 1955, the Burlington's 18 2-10-4 locomotives were commonly seen rolling tonnage across the Iowa countryside when they were finally bumped off of the east-west mainline and sent back to the Illinois coal lines. When working across Iowa, the big M-4As would be seen in fast freight service and even on passenger specials and mail extras. Built by Baldwin Locomotive Works in December 1927, and modified to M-4A specifications by the shop crew at West Burlington in November 1939, M-4A #6317 is moving light through the yard at Pacific Junction. The date is October 7, 1952 and in less than three years #6317 will be again working on the Beardstown Division south of Galesburg. *(Don Ball collection)*

St. Joseph to Pacific Junction
TIME TABLE No. 68.

Mile Post Locations	STATIONS (112.47)	Distances from St. Joseph Freight Yards (Miles)	Capacity of Northward Siding	Capacity of Other Tracks
60.15	ST. JOSEPH FRT. YDS.		Yard	Yard
	—1.30—			
	U. P. Crossing (Grade) C. R. I. & P. Crossing (Grade)			
	—0.20—			
61.75	ST. JOSEPH U. S.	1.50	Yard	Yard
	—0.20—			
	M. P. Crossing (Grade)			
	—0.60—			
64.01	FRANCIS STREET U. T. Crossing (Interlocked)	2.30		
	—2.89—			
66.90	WATER WORKS	5.19		18
	—5.26—			
72.16	AMAZONIA	10.45	80	13
	—4.87—			
77.03	NODAWAY	15.32		7
	—6.25—			
83.28	FORBES	21.57		23
	—8.24—			
91.52	FOREST CITY	29.81	75	62
	—5.90—			
97.42	NAPIER	35.71	81	155
	—4.46—			
101.88	BIGELOW	40.17	75	29
	—7.39—			
109.27	CRAIG	17.56	125	29
	—5.71—			
114.98	CORNING	53.27	125	50
	—4.41—			
119.39	NISHNABOTNA	57.68	83	27
	—6.57—			
124.96	LANGDON	63.25	61	24
	—3.29—			
128.25	PHELPS	66.54	70	24
	—6.53—			
133.78	WATSON	72.07	125	23
	—8.22—			
142.00	HAMBURG	80.29	87	108
	—7.25—			
149.25	PAYNE	87.54	125	22
	—6.36—			
155.61	PERCIVAL	93.90	69	28
	—5.02—			
160.63	McPAUL	98.92	125	18
	—4.49—			
165.12	BARTLETT	103.41	68	16
	—9.06—			
174.18	PACIFIC JUNCTION C. B. & Q. Crossing (Interl.)	112.47	Yard	Yard

(Above) Twenty three years after being built by Baldwin, Class O-5A #5602, the third 4-8-4 to enter service on the Burlington, is seen on the ready track at "P. Junc." The cab signal equipment and Mars light were brand new when this photo was taken on March 17, 1953. *(Bob Bullermann collection)*

(Below) Five EMD F-units, led by F-3A #122D, are ample power for the hottest freight on the system, the Chicago-Denver CD. After a brief stop at the yard office for a crew change, the CD will rumble across the diamond with the Council Bluffs/Kansas City line and head west into the sunset and on to Denver, where it is scheduled to arrive at 11:15 the next morning. The date is May 30, 1959, and the locomotives supplying the CD with 7,500 hp are F-3A #122A, F-3B #122B, F-3B #166B, F-3B #130B and F-3A #130A. *(M. Spoor collection)*

Council Bluffs

During the 1860s and 1870s, a number of railroads pushed westward across Iowa aiming for the important railhead of Omaha. The Burlington had reached Pacific Junction in November 1869. The Kansas City, St. Joseph and Council Bluffs Rail Road, closely aligned with the Burlington and eventually consolidated into the CB&Q, had reached Council Bluffs in 1867. Regular service across Iowa from Burlington to Council Bluffs began on January 1, 1870.

(Above) The CB&Q tracks stopped in Council Bluffs so trains continuing on to Omaha on the west bank of the Missouri River would utilize trackage rights on the Union Pacific to cross the river. On September 7, 1957, CB&Q Northern #5632 storms west out of Council Bluffs on Union Pacific trackage with a short freight, and in a few minutes will be crossing the Missouri River. When it reaches CB&Q tracks it will be operating on the Lincoln Division and "Lines West." Converted to burn oil instead of coal, #5632 had been reclassified as an O-5B. *(Lou Schmitz)*

America's Distinctive Trains

(Above) The Burlington's engine facilities in Council Bluffs were modest, consisting of a small roundhouse, coaling tower and 80' turntable. In June 1963, SW-1 #9141 was parked on one of the tracks next to the roundhouse. The Rock Island depot is in the background. *(F. Hol Wagner, Jr.)*

(Below) F-2A #153, awaiting the next call to duty, idles on the ready track at the engine facility in this June 1964 photo. The shabby appearance of the unit is understandable since it is scheduled to be stricken from the roster by the end of the month and traded in on a new GP-35. *(Lloyd Keyser)*

By 1957 the sun will have all but set on active steam in revenue service on "Lines East" on the Burlington. The M-4As were still to be found laboring on the Beardstown Division and an occassional O-1A was working at Herrin Junction. During the second half of the 1950s the ZEPHYR fleet is in its heyday, diesels will have replaced the iron horse and in 1958 the railroad will adopt a bold new paint scheme for its stable of second generation diesel locomotives. Burlington President Harry Murphy will pay homage to the road's steam locomotive heritage by sponsoring numerous steam excursions throughout the 1950s and early 1960s over most of the trackage that comprises "Lines East." All this and more will be covered in *CHICAGO BURLINGTON AND QUINCY In Color, Volume 2*.

Sunset at Western Springs, Illinois. *(George Speir)*

Way of the Zephyrs